Equitable... Insanity!

Dave Lord

authorHOUSE®

AuthorHouse™
1663 Liberty Drive
Bloomington, IN 47403
www.authorhouse.com
Phone: 1-800-839-8640

First published by AuthorHouse 1/10/2011

ISBN: 978-1-4567-1336-2 (e)
ISBN: 978-1-4567-1337-9 (sc)

Library of Congress Control Number: 2010918450

Printed in the United States of America

Contents

A Broken heart. . .

You can hold a broken heart together for a time,
Before the pain overwhelms,
You can only trust a foolish lie, before the truth tells,
Imagination only works in a fairy tale,
Make believe is considered until the age of 12,
Then the pain is more compressed,
Then the tears are real, the mind becomes depressed,
You learn love lost its thrill, though you try to hide the stress,
You know what you feel, sometimes you cannot breathe,
Your cheeks hold the trace, the wound, you bleed,
Sad is on your face, you look for happiness to embrace,
Try to understand the hurt felt, search inside, scrutiny,
Come to realize it's from insecurities, some owned by you,
Some by your partner, lust was the glue, that always falters,
Once the dreams kept you alive, now wondering how to survive,
But a new day prevails, yesterdays gone, drink from the well of carry on,
The morning comes the sun will rise, a sparkle of hope within the eyes,
New ideas begin to form, another heart to keep you warm,
Plans for tomorrow start to fit, the tears and the sorrow seem to quit,
The will to move forward takes control,
The past forgotten, don't care, don't know…

Author…Dave Lord

Age. . .

Age is the number of our lives
Mind does not understand
While the body's getting older
Mind, wills to survive
Life cannot expand
Wish, the body bolder
Questions as time ticks
Where the years go?
Ever, as it sickens
Mind never knows
Year upon year
What is the trick?
Help to weather
Build upon the brick
Age is the number
Buried in with time
Minds simply slumber
Resists the real, denies…

Author…Dave Lord

A Rainbow. . .

Search for a rainbow on a cloudy afternoon,
Calling for a storm in the middle of June,
Hoping for the sun to shine,
Pot of gold or just a dime,
Patience, until next time,
Comes darkness in the mind,
Silenced, no one will see, violence is the color,
Temple is complete, violins utter,
In a straw hat, farmer plow the fields,
Plant the seeds of wheat,
Don't look back, or yield,
Bake some bread to eat,
I'm not my neighbor's keeper, they're vacationing,
They will return, sometime in the spring,
Hold to the future, the past has failed to try,
Fade to mature, sweet buy…and buy…,
Work the night shift, sleep all day,
Get to make a living, die in distant gray,
Who will appreciate the red, the green, the indigo?
If you can't provide, where is the rainbow?
Coward there you hide, orange and yellow and blue,
Sense of inner self, guide the mystic truth,
Get a coat its cold outside, snow begins to fall,
A dismal afternoon,
Catch a ride, baby learns to crawl,
A man on the moon,
Watch a TV show,
While waiting…on the rainbow…

Author…Dave Lord

Absolute. . .

Near the door of absolute, waiting to get in,
Suddenly hear it close, maybe from the wind,
So I stand outside, the rain joins my tears,
Hoping just to be with you, the hours disappear,
Day is falling and dark is rushing in,
My heart is calling, drink the shot of gin,
Begging time to slow, sad in me begins,
Why can't I touch you, I long for your embrace?
The world runs through and steals my chance away,
Plans shattered my moments of faith,
Will scattered, searching for grace,
Lifeless, my hands fall to the side,
Shoulders slump, hang my head to cry,
Turn my eyes toward heaven in despair,
Filled with passion, I just want to be there,
To see you smile, to hold you in my arms,
To touch an angel, elude stress filled harm,
From every day pressure, the weight crashing,
The oceans storm, the waves thrashing,
The calm peacefulness, held within your eyes,
The sad lifts, happiness arrives,
Sweet blissfulness, chills down my back,
Surrender unto it, sense of relax,
For a little while, quest let it be,
Timeless, lovable, harmony…

Author…Dave Lord

Acceptance. . .

Accept not what others say
For then it becomes you
Reject it then cast it away
Believe your own truths
For if the claim is of anger
It is themselves whom they hate
And place it to others
Themselves they won't face
View your own heart
Reflect what is real
Promote the beautiful
Then who can conceal
Opinions of others
Are futile at best
Shrug your shoulders
And lay it to rest
Discard the lies
Of those who guess
Energy, do not invest
Who knows you more than yourself?
Allow not then anyone else
To commit you to less then you are
Let heal, the pain, the harm
You're part of the universal repertoire

Author...Dave Lord

Afraid to Be!

Afraid to be rejected
Afraid to be alone
Self-disrespected
Afraid of the unknown
A fear of hurting others
Afraid of hurt, yourself
You put you 2nd to everyone else
Afraid to be a failure
A fear of success
Accept mediocre, inside depressed
Always ever trying, proof you can win
To self, unsatisfying, where does one begin?
Look for escape routes
Find an open door
Climb into your clown suit
Laughing at the chore
Wash into career, broken are the dreams
Wish and hope returned, you've met the common needs
Hide from ambition, damn the inner want
Slow anticipation, Time the passing taunt
First you are too young, 'do what you are told'
Then comes age, you find yourself too old
Afraid of winning a life of ecstasy
Sin filled worries practiced carefully
Mysterious, your courage, living in safety
Renowned journey…afraid to be!

Author…Dave Lord

Age defines the innocence. . .

Age defines the innocence, you'll find as you grow,
When you are little, of what do you know?
Teenage, you learn what is taught,
Pushing limits hoping not to be caught,
Then life turns to lust and important things,
Pressing forward against the wings,
Try to take flight, compete for the gold,
Before you realize you're getting old,
Suddenly that promotion or the training class,
Holds less excitement, more a pain in the ass,
What seemed important yesterday,
Is one thing more you cast away,
Not from lack of caring, not because you've quit,
But you learn the art of survival and just don't give a shit, Tomorrow will come
whether you want it or not,
Just another struggle, life against the odds,
You stand behind the shield, dodge the brigade,
Hoping the bullets won't ricochet,
And you catch one as a fatal wound,
Night can't come to fast or to soon,
Then you hide inside the fortress, prepare for a new day,
Put up your guard, trying hard to not be slain...

Author...Dave Lord

Aged. . .

On or about 85, if we make it that far,
Sitting at the local diner, belly up to the bar,
Talking, but not saying much,
Just 2 friends, keeping in touch,
Complaining of illness or about the weather,
A long standing friendship still together,
Enjoy the breakfast that we order,
Reminiscing, hear the laughter,
Wondering, how long we have,
Who would send off whom?
Grab our canes, still gabbing,
As we shuffle out of the room,
'See you next week', say our good byes,
Drive into the street, wipe our eyes,
Waving, grins on our cheeks,
Anxious already for this time to repeat,
Headed back to our lonely spaces,
Dreaming still of better places,
Children's hopes, wished sensations,
Treat the time line with motivation,
Success or fail no obligation,
Kiss and tell, love is the need,
Friend to friend, neighbor to neighbor,
Parent to child, husband and wife,
Lover to lover,
There is effort, sometimes labor,
Learn to smile with life,
Always be faithful and believe,
Live each day with pleasure…

Author…Dave Lord

Alive. . .

Starving to live, dying to survive
Believing the truth where's a disguise
Knowing every lie upon lie
No more feeling alive
Cover reality with happy thoughts
More frustration is all it has brought
Hoping for better opportunities
While the world crumbles beneath
Knowing the economic tragedies
Wishing for more, is like a disease
Burrowing in to the midst of the soul
Eating away leaving a hole
Dreaming a life, wanting to be
Wasting away from reality
Plan for the future prepare for a fight
We have ruptured the suture
In the middle of the night
One, which had sewn peace together
Burst open wide, angered leather
Like a whip snap, the pain we feel
Is one of a worldwide ordeal
Looking to government to feed the masses
Forcing ourselves, to see through rose glasses
Nation upon nation owning the fright
Of how to live on, in this hellish plight
Fingers pointing, hate levels high

All pray to God, that they should survive
Willing to fire in a blink of an eye
Guns blazing, no fears to die
Bombs exploding, a smoke filled sky
At the end of the battle, the bitter sweet cries
Those left standing to claim their prize
A world devastated of mad ignorance
Worry the effects of the consequence
Millions left bleeding, deaths rotting flesh
Due to the greedy wretch
Famine causes more life to fall
God help us, God help us, one and all…

Author…
Dave Lord

Searching. . .

All of us searching
Who we are
Reaching for what we wish to be
Failing more often than not
Wondering our purpose
Tunnel vision...the goal, so far
Success only imagined
Yet, at the end I see a light
Shining, with a reflection
Notice, the image...I recognize
There is my destination
Growing up, that is who I hoped to be
The dreams, plans, expectations...shuffled by life
Careers, children, change...time
Fear, insecurities...survival took over my mind
Still, the reflection stares back
Closer...now plain I see
The one in the reflection, smiles...
That one is me...

Author
David Lord

Angels. . .

Angel's wings spread to fly,
Innocence, believes the lies,
Learning what life's about,
Still unknown, the endless doubt,
Angel's wings, heart is whole,
Welcoming what the futures hold,

Angels wings more heavy laden,
Unsure of life's task,
Understands life's more blatant,
Gripping to the flask,
Where once wished to fly,
Disbelief makes one shy,

Angel's wings black as coal,
Deep within the darkened soul,
Pain and hurt, reality,
Hides the wings, propriety,

Angel's wings to weak to fly,
Heavy burdened, seeks the sky,
All of life's tragedies, brings the soul to its knees,
Broken by the secret minds, learning truths become the lies,
Wondering of life's content, all energy of life was spent,
Wishing on angels wings, broken promise which evil brings,
Certainty is justified, once the angels wings have died…

Author…Dave Lord

Another day. . .

Another day, get in my truck and drive,
A hundred eighty miles before I arrive,
Cup of coffee, fill the tank, an ATM receipt,
That would be the life line, to know if I can eat,
$45.00 before I hit the red,
Paycheck in 3 days, hanging by a thread,
Ride the un-tolled roads, them I can't afford,
Grateful to be working, economy's been gored,
Stomachs getting hungry, food I packed is gone,
Snacks behind me, got to last on,
Items from the dollar store, how I survive,
Nutrition's out the window, but I stay alive,
Though I have shelter, I live inside a house,
Nothing is mine, reminds my loving spouse,
I'm just in existence, finances are in shreds,
Since I've moved here, they've worsened instead,
Pay a monthly rent, pay my bills,
Cell phone and insurance, not much left for frills,
Then to be announced, 'supply your groceries'
Breakfast, lunch and dinner, such atrocity,
Cereal and toast, if the kids don't take,
Cold cuts for my sandwiches, lunch and dinner made,
Yet in 16 hours sometimes I'll need more,
Then I'm headed back to the dollar store,
$30.00 left, a few more things to eat,
No I'm not a quitter, refusing defeat,
There shall come a moment when I'll succeed,
Once the day is thrown, beyond just alive,
I'll smile on the days when I survived!

Another Day Lord

Another Night. . .

Another night, running away, in this stale room,
TV in the background, noise of local doom,
Perched upon this bar stool, no one recognized,
Just 2 girls playing pool and 4 guys,
As the hours pass, staring at the bottom of the glass,
Feeling sorry, waiting for pity, bar maid pours another beer,
I look to her for conversation, she doesn't really care,
Bored with this frustration, I head out of there,
Climb into the truck, eyes glazed, radios blaring 'Purple haze',
Wondering what brings me to this place,
See the image, age upon my face,
Successfully losing at this game of life, begging to be sacrificed,
Troubled worry consuming me,
Petrified, where is free, tracking the futile relationships,
My wallet knows the strain, searching accomplishments,
Depression remains, fighting just to be,
Up against the wall, longing for the oceans breeze,
Can not hear its call…Who, does one turn to for leadership?
Greed makes for betrayal, wanted the amenities,
Structure is too frail, breathe an empty sigh,
Reflection, the blanked look,
Mirrors never lie, youth, the years took,
Sense the feel of misery, Felt unpleasant hell,
Take away the enemy, Turn against myself, seeking a path,
Opening the text, learn the simple response,
Take just one more glance, words there are printed,
Penned upon the page, something not hidden,
Told throughout the age,
There between the lines, of what Jesus said,
'I never stopped loving you…<u>you did!</u>'

Author…Dave Lord

Apologize. . .

I no longer apologize for how I live,
I need not ask you to forgive,
You judge me for the job I do,
When the jealous one is you,
I can't apologize for the freedom I own,
You trapped in your institution,
Year after year decades drift by,
Working harder working longer,
Promoted to the next level of insanity,
In the same building, behind those 4 walls,
Maybe the next floor or new cubical,
Where my floor is the road, my ceiling is the sky,
My walls are the trees; everywhere I go a new destiny,
I understand why, your anger I see, I allowed to travel,
Destination unknown, another location to roam,
Freedoms complexity, caged sincerity,
One held captive, excused in ones self, one holds liberty, the spell,
One gives years to the life, one gives life to the years,
No more insensitive, no more will I lie,
Accepting for what it is, my need to do or die…

Author…Dave Lord

Another night calling. . .

Another night calling, silently,
Day is falling quietly,
Travel home from the job,
Hoping chance to see,
Once passed this mob,
A vision of certainty,
Cancel stress and urgency,
Sense the smell of jealousy,
Press upon the mouth the taste of sweet,
Hear the tension as I breathe,
Feel the passions imagery,
As the world fades notably,
Angels test majestically, burn desires instantly,
Confess to some degree, acknowledged, the heart does beat,
Enter through sheer beauty,
Touch the hand carefully,
Mind seeks make believe, souls synchronize,
Smiles form in the eyes, joy sings triumphantly,
Trace the tear less recognized, fear surrenders violently,
Hell gives in to heavenly, freedom is the courtesy,
Blindness sells to good bye, arms around the love concede,
Torment now tragically, dies to lust under blue skies,
Here next to me, life repeatedly, comes to no surprise...

Author...Dave Lord

16

Ascending. . .

Sitting in the park
On a warm summers eve
Enjoying the coolness
From the days humidity
As I look toward the stars
And gazed at the sky
A sight from the grass
Catches my eyes
Fireflies ascending
From the ground to the air
I wondered, as I sat and stared
Ascending to heaven
Would it be this way?
When our Lord calls us
On that faithful day
The day of his return
The day he's coming back
Then, I worried of my soul
Was it ugly and black?
So, I knelt down before him
With tears on my face
Asked forgiveness for my fall from grace
Prayed for his guidance
Till the day of recognition
For like the lightening bugs before me
I may join in the ascension…

Author
Dave Lord

Appointment. . .

I have an appointment
Yet, I'm not sure when
My patience, disappointing
Rescheduled again
Waiting for a turn
When will it be?
This appointment is trying me
Maybe that is the issue
I'm looking at myself
Wanting my turn
To blind to see
Others may require
A problem of greater need
I suppose then, I can wait
I have time; it's not too late
I'm still here, getting along
I'm happy that I belong
In line, I'll have to stand
Waiting for my demands
It's all right, each step I trod
One step closer to my appointment with God...

Author
Dave Lord

Ashes to ashes. . .

Ashes to ashes, dust to dust,
Formed from matter, in God we trust,
Born on earth, live till death,
Seek rebirth, in our heads,
Fears and passion, selfish ego,
Greed and gnashing, win, place, or show,
Searching for a tear, reaching for the sky,
Drunk on beer and apple pie,
Time is urgently ticking,
Heart of a child, thoughts of a man,
Mind always clicking, buy the mini van,
Life is good, little girl crying,
Misunderstood, the dog is dying,
Cursed are the blessings, women rehearse,
Minutes are wasting, see the new purse,
Its cold on the 4th of July, fireworks blaze,
It is warm on Christmas, confused are days,
7 continents, 7 seals in the bible,
There are no constants, in the world of survival,
Who is he which can endure,
Where is the innocent pure?
Justice forever be still,
Bring in the firsts, for their fill,
Eat of the bounty, at the buffet,
Signs that the country is worn and slain,
Build another ritzy hotel, no one can afford,
Hire employees, dig the well; luck is the world's chore…

Author…Dave Lord

Atlantic City. . .

Atlantic City, its midnight, drive to the Taj Mahal,
You, I invite, deserving it all,
Walk the boardwalk, hear the oceans waves,
Bright lights and small talk, the senses cave,
Bent across the table, Texas hold em,
We start to gamble, excitement,
Two faced down, I hold a pair,
Lick the lips as I stare,
The queen of hearts lying there,
An ace, quite beautiful,
I raise, intense emotions,
I'm all in, wonderful sensations,
On the table a ten,
Silence crowds the room, heavy breathing heard,
The scent of perfume, passion, is the verb,
There on its back, lays a jack,
Concerned, in your hand, is there a king?
I squeeze my pair, wondering, I jerk, my drink spills,
Splashes on your cheek, hoping you'll react then I'll get a peek,
Not about the money, it's about the game,
Will the pair I hold win the heart again?
I flip my cards; a pair of tens, the one on the table makes 3
A king in your hand makes a straight,
Bloods pumping, could it be,
Who will win, the silence breaks,
You scream 'I fold', your voice quivers,
Your drink drips down your lap,
Chills down my back, shiver,
The card your hand still holds,
The king of hearts match the rest, the nights a quiet hush,
You threw your cards to end the game, but held a Royal Flush...

Author...Dave Lord

Awake. . .

Awake to the noise, take the morning pill,
Drive the crooked road, wash away the will,
The sentence awaits, drink of what is spilled,
Another cup of coffee, as the hours drag,
The year is nearly over, breakfast in a bag,
Sigh, alone together, hate is all you feel,
Love will last forever, life's a fairytale,
Seek some compassion, no ones standing there,
Heat the cold a fraction, know the dead blank stare,
Reaching for the wallet, head out to the bar,
'I'll be home by 8',
Found another lover, last name is Walker,
A shot of red, a shot of black,
A few shots more, headed back,
Key inside the lock turn left and right,
Door doesn't open, ready for a fight,
In a world of distant losers, hear the beating drum,
Fist upon the door, pain a broken thumb,
Wonder of the crime and why the punishment,
Emotionally numb, Saints repent,
Clouded by the reasons, lawyers on the phone,
Understanding treason, breached and over thrown,
Pack the suitcase, smell the sexual sleaze,
Confirmed by your neighbor, infidelity,
Tense the situation, spit upon the tree,
Inside the sounds echoing, born free,
Silence of the still, break captivity,
Emptiness fulfilled, senseless tragedy,
Prison is the cell, warden by the gate…

Author – Dave Lord

Beach. . .

Walking on the beach feel the oceans mist,
Sounds of the surf, day turns to dusk,
Air a little brisk, yet the time worth,
Moments last forever, hours we're together,
Watch the moon rise, on the oceans tide,
Head back to our room dress for warm,
Go and walk the boards,
Hand in hand taking in the sights,
Soon return to spend the night, ready for bed under the sheets,
Understand no one will sleep, watch as the sun kisses the horizon,
Breakfast awaits let's go buy some,
Back to the sand eyes close, awake later sunscreen the nose,
Turn, enjoy the relaxation, happy with you, sweet sensation…

Author…Dave Lord

Beautiful One. . .

You are the beautiful, care to let me in,
For I am the dutiful, temptress of the sin,
Eyes of crystal, silk is your skin,
As a rose pedal, beauty within,
Sexual incantation, breathless, there you are,
You control the spell, whether near or far,
Daily the thought, ever bring you nigh,
Wars have been fought, for such exquisiteness, by and by,
So attractive, this woman of splendor,
Magnificent, glorious, grandeur,
Ever always elegant bravura, dazzling hearts and minds,
Personality, fine charisma, pleasant aura revealed,
Constant wanting, to allure, I try…
This virtuoso, mesmerized and enthralled,
Fascination you've become,
Power of magnetism,
Persuades, one on one…

Author…Dave Lord

Beauty is a talent. . .

Beauty is a talent, time does erase,
Dance to the music, lines upon the face,
Stake in the chest, vanquish the best,
Beauty is its own enemy, valued is the sight,
Better scene at night,
Make up becomes your only friend,
Once heads would turn,
Youth builds the urn
As age shows vanity,
Welcomed to the thrill,
The drink which you just spilled,
Bless the cursed world to its knees,
Juggle emptiness, loves a passing glance,
Take what is offered at the door,
Eternal beauty is the chore,
Break the egg of summer's heat,
Check the calories before you eat,
Listen to the insults, seen by repulsive eyes,
Terror harms the results, chill runs down the spine,
Morning paint the canvas, greet the new days madness,
Spark the match to let them see, stroke the brush upon it,
Trace the shrewdness of joviality, fake laughter, then to spit,
Earned the talent of beauty…

Author…Dave Lord

Behind. . .

Behind the door of yesterday, of what used to be,
There lie the things I can't control, it's all history,
Today is that, of which I need concern,
And tomorrow, of which I will learn,
I've danced among the flowers,
I danced among the trees,
I've felt an April shower,
I hear and I can see,
I worked at my career,
I have a family,
I don't have millions,
When it comes to cash,
But I've always had enough,
I've found time to laugh,
And sometimes had some tough,
Yet overall I look and what I perceive,
Of this world I know, life's been good to me…

Author…Dave Lord

Big Blue Dot. . .

Big blue dot, photo from afar,
In the universe just another star,
As shown by scientists, yet is it true,
Or should we believe of the crucified Jew?
Which have not lies? Neither says I,
For man cannot speak the truth,
Therefore are they not both uncouth,
Did we really land on the moon, or was it a film on the desert?
Could aliens be assumed, or does arrogance perverse,
To think we are alone, how does an angel remove a stone?
Microscopic organism lay upon the sheets,
Shake them and destroy an entire colony,
A planet explodes light years away; could **this** star be next on any given day?
But God loves us of his own accord, do you not believe in the holy word?
I say of the 2 understandings I have heard,
I must believe, for it's the least absurd,
Yet words have been written and tales have been told,
Mistakes have been proven and liars are of old,
Thus stories have been spoken and exaggerations have construed,
Then misunderstandings one cannot elude,
Johnny picked an apple and gave it to a girl,
Till that stories finished, Johnny owns the world,
Adding to the mystery, dramatic affect,
So the question is, is the bible correct?
In 7 days God creates the earth,
Missing from the pages are the dinosaurs,
God created Adam, from his rib came Eve,
I know I have one less, than the woman next to me,
There's the proof now take a stand,
Why is there no mention of the caveman?
Look upon the tree and touch upon the leaf,
See the new born baby, take another breath,
Ah, because you can, there seems to be enough for every human,
Ink the finger tip press it to the page,
10 different ones for all who have lived,
Quite the database, whoever gets to give,
Individuality, intellectual, confused, technical,

I guess for the course this must be par,
Then there's the concept of the calendar,
When was that created, and who placed on the days?
Was it not Caesar in the Roman games?
If a day is a year and a year is a day,
Wouldn't this be contradictory per say?
God owns no calendar he is timeless,
Maybe its there hence we conceive this,
We cannot envisage the greater divine, to believe is easier I find,
So of a God there must be, He is much greater than thee,
Of life eternally, I pray, let it be,
But the curse and pain of hell, the place where Satan dwells,
May it be of life itself, let love not fear excel,
Bless the poorest man and the one, who owns the land,
Since life is all in vain, who is not and who is sane,
Reach a helping hand, strap on the watches band,
As time thus ticks away, forgive us lord I pray…

Author…Dave Lord

Blinded. . .

Blinded by the sight, obviously,
No living man will resist,
One woman with so much beauty,
Proves angels exist,
Entering the room, eyes turn and stare,
Smiles replace the gloom,
Knowing her presence there,
Noting, sensuality is way beyond compare,
Blessed by loveliness, jealousy everywhere,
Sweet personality, stunning, voluptuous,
Scent of lust fills the air,
Perfection seen, by those who can,
Otherwise, call a priest,
Last rights for the dying man,
Men who were confused,
Once they get a glimpse,
Turn from what they knew,
No man slips her grip,
Women who sought men, no longer they're sure,
He who holds the pen is of what they allure,
Once this beauty exits,
All begin to breathe,
Saints be praised and kisses,
Precious is she…

Author…Dave Lord

Brain washed. . .

Turned on the radio to hear some music,
Started pushing the scan button pretty quick,
'Buy a new mattress to get better rest,
Get your house from us, we sell the best,
Then caught the news, earthquake in Chile,
Unemployment is up, help Haiti,
Expect a hike at the pump,
Buy our internet protection; the Dow is down bad sales projection,
We have the best cut diamonds she wants, come eat at our restaurant,
Thirsty, we have coffee, only a dollar a cup,
Purchase candy or a doughnut,
Donate your money to help our cause, we have a sale,
Wish you were here, come visit, buy our brand of ale,
Time for a new car we have them all, won't see this price again till fall, Better your
business advertise here, only $2000 a year,
Need new tires or an oil change, stop by and we'll arrange,
How about a soda, buy one get one free,
A new Dodge Dakota will make you happy,
Jesus saves call in your prayer; please send your money for our savior,
Spend the night with us, get a free breakfast,
Shop here and save with coupons, get your pizza and say 'Hi' to John,
Cloudy today, traffic jam, stop for eggs and ham
Or a bowl of soup, it might snow, time to ski
Come on up and spend your money,
We are here stop by our store,'
Alright, I can't take anymore,
Finally, a song by that singer Josh,

No, I don't think we're brain washed...

Author Dan Lad

Breathe. . .

The more I breathe; love seeks to deafen me,
The more I bleed; I know I'm not the enemy,
Will you grieve, have I become the sheep
Shall I leave, pull the sword from its sheath,
Blind to faith, hell bounds constantly,
Release the rage, revenge now set free…

Author…Dave Lord

Breathless. . .

Breathless, I become whenever you are near
Timeless, others numb, your beauty ever clear
Speechless, words succumb, my tongue it cannot steer
Endless, moments drum and quickly disappear
Ageless, if I won, my wish the stars would hear
Dime less is the sum, my wallet ever fears
Worthless, are those funds, if you they're not aware
Jealous, I am one, "Just for me" I cheer
Care less, none... you bring life to these, my dear....

Author...Dave Lord

Bright the sun. . ..

Bright the sun and green the grass clear the sky of blue,
Every morn and every eve my mind it thinks of you,
Gray the clouds and rain does fall, cold and damp and wet,
Still my thoughts can't control wanting you yet,
In the place I am or where I am to be,
Every where I go, I wish you there with me,
Atop the highest mountain, or lying at the beach,
I just want you, close enough to reach,
This spell that I am under, mystic as the wind,
Blows from east to west, then south to north,
Beneath the star lit night it blows my ship off course,
And though my thoughts quixotic,
I will not waste this dream, my soul is aquatic,
Believes in the extreme, thus days will come upon us,
And life will soon begin, the world no longer unjust,
Our hearts will trust passion, and see the gracious scent,
Recognized together vehement...

Author...Dave Lord

Broken promises. . .

Broken promises forgotten dreams
For ones selfishness, for ones needs
Not considered, the others pleas
Broken promises forgotten dreams
Vows were taken, longevity
Their mistaken activities
Each together a few hours a night
Separated throughout the days light
Complicated by life itself
Money, careers, children, what else?
Stress between them too much
Missing, the lovers touch
Broken promises forgotten dreams
Emotionally upon your knees
Sparked for a second
Lived for a moment
Lack of commitment
The largest component
Broken promises forgotten dreams
Sorrow, sadness…return the keys
House is empty, sale is pending
Live to fast, love now ending…

Author
Dave Lord

Buddy L

I remember a time when I was small
getting a gift at Christmas
I tore open the package and saw, 'Buddy L'
I yelled, "Help me with this"
when it was out of the box
the excitement I held inside
screamed out, I was shocked
no more, the excitement would hide
a station wagon, long and green
4 doors, I opened them all
the detail was so extreme
"Thanks, Mom and Dad" I called
Tires of rubber, each wheel had a spring
the roof rack and numbers
Chrome plating
license plate, bumpers
wood grain and a working rear window and door
"Thanks, Mom and Dad...I won't need anything more"...

Author
David Lord

Bullied. . .

Growing up is difficult to say the least,
But it becomes harder when you're bullied,
Instruction, direction, fears to behave,
Come from your parents on a given day,
'Don't let me hear you got in a fight',
Quickly you learn to hide inside,
Preyed upon because you're weaker,
Bullies make your time bleaker,
Make remarks of hitting you, and then say it's in jest,
When no one is looking, fist into your chest,
Soon you become someone you never meant to be,
Acting in ways differently, learn to be cool,
Find your friends and hang,
In numbers there's protection, ask any gang,
Lifting weights, boxing, trying to be tough,
Create a reputation you've had enough,
Day after day it's just survive, at the end of each, glad you're alive,
When a fight is inevitable, but you walk away,
You quickly join your friends just to say,
He wasn't worth it, I'm better than that,
While your heart pounds, worry of a heart attack,
But deep inside you feel the coward,
To yourself, you start to scowl,
Your friends reaction sour, some throw in the towel,
Years pass and you're more mature, but something inward eats away,
Anger more obscure, 'you they will obey',
Distance is your friend, running from yourself,
The anger pours out on everybody else,
Unsure how to take control, hate bores in and roots your soul,
Temper often flies, now you hold the fear,
Each day you live the lie, you're equal to your peers,
You want to respect yourself, you cannot give,

Author...Dave Lord

Captivated. . .

Captivated by my own fear,
Living as though I'm free,
Waiting the miracle year after year,
Learning the fool is me,
Miracles won't happen upon a wish,
Dreams form in the unconscious,
I've seen the selfishness,
Know of the pompous,
Lived in the bitterness,
Know the will of pertinacious,
Though I've settled for the less,
Though I've given in,
Submitted to the ignorance,
No more, I stand to win,
So bring forth the enemy,
Take upon your sword,
Remove this tyranny, end this war,
Prepare to fight the battle,
Assure the consequence,
For high upon the saddle,
Ready for the offense,
Blood for blood, screams shall be heard,
Love undone, sadness in a word,
But life replenished, game of the absurd,
Conquered living, no longer in a cell,
Chance forgiving, escaped my own hell...

Author...Dave Lord

Care

I watch the night cover the sky
In the distance I see a tear in your eye
The one within you deep inside
You wear the smile because of pride
You will not grieve the hurt you feel
Instead you wear a false armor of steal
Why face the hurt, why face the pain
There is nothing much to be gained
Yet, each experience is a part of living
Learn from them and be forgiving
We all must slowly take each step
Before we grow, before we get
Rewards for learning from the mistakes we've made
A love true, our soul saved
Sometimes until we reach that place
Some hurt, some pain must be faced
And then the tears won't continue to fall
The smile no longer will be false
You'll move on to another day
One less mistake in your way…

Author
David Lord

Celebrate. . .

Passion, pierce the gratefulness, fill the empty soul,
Wish to own peacefulness, these cards suck, I fold,
Help save that child, blessings to the whore,
Fashion is the style, knock the opened door,
Celebrate the birthday, celebrate life,
Celebrate death, just to be nice,
Then after time, they're a memory,
To those they have touched, for the time they breathe,
Generations passing, perform expected deeds,
Once before the alter, the common man shall bleed,
Diamonds are forever, until love enters in,
Then the diamonds luster, fails to begin,
Shake the muddy water; stir the cup of tea,
Until there is no difference, for the mortal man to see,
Vines upon the mansions, windows broken through,
Money is the pit fall, if we only knew,
All of us pushing, so hard, we try,
One must ask the question, who knows why?
Stuck on the freeway, traffic jam ahead,
Fear the ultimatum, jobless, broke, unfed,
Chance to win the lottery, the old lady fell,
Chance that someone cares, when it snows in hell,
Can you reach the limit, before you grow too old?
Youth is more committed, lessons, the unknown,
Worthless endeavor on a distant shore,
600 billion dollars, no money for the poor,
Sun sets in the West, past the smoke and flames,
Was the sun once a planet filled with this insane?

Food seems plentiful, ever wonder how,
Abuse is so intense; it would raise your eyebrows,
Where the waters flooding, no one can drink,
A drought gets them running, note those of extinct,
Fly the plane from where you sit, across the 7 seas,
GPS scans through space, thanks technology,
Global economics, one world government,
Big brother knows where you are, before you ever went,
Microchips are now placed in dogs, so they can't be lost,
Soon it will be humans, who shall bare the costs,
Homeless on the corner, scrape by to eat,
Listen to the preaching, the bible is complete,
Welcome all the news, worlds' determination,
I wonder how soon, we'll fulfill Revelations?

Author...Dave Lord

Christmas. . .

Well the day has arrived; the gifts are all wrapped,
The tree decorated, the house trimmed in lights,
Credit cards inflated, Santa comes tonight,
But this year is different, I see from afar,
Like the wise men watching Bethlehem's star,
You see my grand baby just turned 1,
The first Christmas the enthusiasm,
That I missed when I was young,
Since my own child separated through divorce
I certainly tried to follow the course
Pressured by job and the bills I had to pay,
I chose to be selfish and look the other way,
Hurry through the season, get this function done,
Who was deprived, I the only one,
To see the excitement in her little eyes,
Her expression from each new surprise,
To see the smile upon her face,
Receive the hug of innocent grace,
That's what it's about, the joy of the season,
The innocent love with the slightest of reason,
Love pure, precious from the cradle,
Love sure, all of us able,
For one day remove all of what life has tossed,
And love like he who bore the cross.

Merry Christmas

Author...Dave Lord

City. . .

Sirens awake me from the extreme,
Gun shots heard outside my door,
Echoed in the night are screams,
I push my children to the floor,
All the wonderment are dreams,
I kneel and beg 'no more',
Who listens to the pleas, a soldier in this war
Though I have no enemies, this place in where I dwell,
This town is the disease; death has its own smell,
And who are those who judge, on my life they label,
The paper bares the smudge, ink poured on the table,
There under the grudge, it states that I am able,
Though eyes cannot see, the force among the stable,
My wage, by some degree, brings me to where I'm at,
Descent air to breathe, is kept for the fat,
Hide with the debris, hope to stay alive,
Dealt then they fell, once more to survive,
Chamber of hell, escaped one more time,
Pour the breakfast, the box eaten through,
Rats from the basement, share the food,
Speak you are living, generally its true,
Satan unforgiving, the battle scars prove,
Another promise spoken, 'soon we shall move',
Again the promise broken, fear held in the eyes,
Children, trust the token, you hold your own lies...

Author...Dave Lord

41

Cliff Hanger...

Hello, I am a cliff hanger
Hanging cliffs on rusty nails
For I know not what I do
I pray they will not fail
For the people beneath the ridge
Would perish, lost heritage
But I convinced those of freewill
Of my talents and my skills
Black ink upon the page
Prejudged by what they've gauged
"He has hung these cliffs before
Unhinged from heavens door
This sheet spells what he can do
Let's bring him on, I implore
He can start the 1st of June"
So I hang these cliffs upon the nails
And test them for support
But as the rain pours in and makes them frail
They may fall from the force
Thus, I hide myself in another place
In hopes they won't recall my face
Share my words of skill and talent
Another cliff lies in the balance
If they fall and lives are lost
Who then should bare the cross?
The laborer, is it I
Or those who believed the lies...

Author...Dave Lord

Cold. . .

Cold the night and silent, quiet filled with sleep,
Peaceful addiction, where is the thrill,
Self allow permission, another glass to fill,
Awaiting perfection, dreams are often spilled,
What is the prediction, fire up the grill,
Touch the distant passion, taste the maple syrup,
Drink in the white Russian, foot in the stir-up,
Climb upon the beast, release, empty the cups,
Latch onto the body, lick upon the lips,
Turn the rider over, reaching for the grips,
Slow the engine, clutch the hand brakes,
Push to the limit; see what it can take,
Drive into the tunnel, seek a destiny,
Dark and damp the funnel, be the fantasy,
Find a gallant love, wisp away the sane,
Helmet on the Harley till you ride again,
You've become the pilot, fear upon the sheets...

Author...Dave Lord

Come Home. . .

'Come home with me, I plan to succeed,
You won't have a need, this my fantasy',
It's all been a dream,
'You won't have to cry, everything I will buy,
I'm yours till I die',
It's all been a lie,
I'll pay every bill; more heat warms the chill,
My mind it's been ill, take just one more pill,
Each day there is strife, divorced my 3rd wife,
This can't be my life, hand me the butchers knife,
I've knelt and I've prayed,
When will I be saved?
I've always behaved, my wishes, I do crave,
I can't clear my head, so much do I dread,
It has all been said, it's like I am dead,
Nothing seems to matter, my bones and teeth chatter,
I fell from Jacobs's ladder; my heart and soul are shattered,
Gave myself to love, but all they do is judge,
Where is the peaceful dove?
I need a stronger drug,
Pour a gin and tonic; drive through at the Sonic,
The cough I have is chronic; they tell me I'm demonic,
Feelings are crushed and hurt; I drown myself in my work,
Once more I avert; all the dreams are in the dirt,
My dreams are in the dirt...

Author...Dave Lord

44

Compassion

Come passion seize the emptiness,
Compassion, completeness,
Fantasy desperate to be,
Come, deliberately,
Heat rising in the night,
Freezing cold outside,
Senses reach justified,
Rudders, ships collide,
Engines race and pistons fire,
In the blocks bored holes,
Tension, rage, instant liars,
Around the block, bored souls,
Naked are the victims,
Tortured by their crime,
Deep inside rejection,
Take another ride,
Feast upon the flesh,
Drill below the spine,
Beast upon the chest,
Drunk within the mind,
Come, passion, swallow,
Sprayed from the hose,
Douse the fire, capture,
Tomorrow judge the woes,
Crush the spirit, jester,
Claims from the wise,
Tears upon the lipstick,
Traced around the eyes,
Bruised beneath the pin prick,
Dark is where you hide,
Stains upon your bed,
Numb and near to death,
Read the scriptures scrolls.
Sexually tainted,
The body, heart of stone,
Angel's wings spread,

On the back, painted,
Love, my God, to own...Love, my God, faded...

Author...Dave Lord

Crouched. . .

Crouched in the corner, blanket on my head,
Seeking the darkness to cover the dead,
Watch the blood run in the street,
See the shells on the ground,
Baffled, hell does repeat
The world fights for the crown,
Bread, water, ammunition,
Lead, laughter, take your position,
Fire upon the crowds, the majority,
Buyers will be proud, new sorority,
Yell and stare at the moon,
Rope off the crime scene,
Sale ends at noon,
University hires a dean,
Break the back of the strong,
Finish, they who are weak,
Fool doesn't belong, soldiers retreat,
Planes and tanks and bombs, irrational calm,
Kiss her rosy red cheek, old man die in your sleep,
'No you can't have a bite', curb your appetite,
Blond hair on the horse, baby pig snorts,
Brisk autumn days, frost here tonight,
Seen the legs x-rays, lost an inch in height,
Bodies on the lake, the sky is simply falling,
Burn the toast; create, another town waltzing,
My paper and my pipe, slippers and my robe,
Tomatoes are to ripe, crack the secret code,
Smoke from the rifle, bullets aimed on high,
Prophets are insightful, science asking why…
Prophets are insightful, science asking why…

Author…Dave Lord

Daddy's Little Girl

A child was born one summer day
A beautiful girl, "I love her" I'd say
Each passing week I'd watch her grow
And my life was all a glow
You'd sit on my lap, we'd watch TV
Or play with a puzzle, or color a tree
You walked and talked so pleasantly
It was hard to believe you were only three
Numbers and letters were easy for you
Shapes and colors, were nothing, it's true
You learned to dress and tie your own shoes
It's no wonder that I love you
Together we'd find a playground somewhere
To swing or slide, while the other kids were there
We'd laugh and play, then home for a nap
I'd be asleep, and you would just clap
Then out for dinner and some Skee ball
Some pizza and Fatz, the funniest of all
The name of the place was called Show Biz
You'd jump in the balls, and I'd play Trivia Quiz
The fun and games would soon go away
I'd take you to mom's house, because that is where you stayed
I'd be quite angry with mom, I confess
Because my house without you just was not blessed
Mommy chose to take you away
But "Soon they'll be home", I'd sit and I'd pray…

Author
Dave Lord

Daughter. . .

Tonight I felt uneasy
As I lay down to sleep
So, I knelt before the savior
And asked 'my soul to keep'
When I finally slumber, Jesus, in a dream
Held me in His arms, as He spoke to me
He said 'Fear not my son for all is in order'
I saw in His eyes, the reflection of my daughter
Waved to me 'Good-Bye'
As she stepped through heavens gate
I began to argue, though in a comforted state
Jesus dried my tears, and held me to His chest
Assured my every fear, and put my pain to rest
He explained, her suffering no more would ever be
In Heaven she'll await, until it's time for me…
In Heaven she'll await, until it's time for me…

Author…Dave Lord

Dedication. . .

Dedication mistaken for disloyalty,
Calm the demons in the mind,
I am not the enemy,
Feel the shivers down your spine,
Though I'm placed upon the alter,
Shall I grieve inside the abattoir?
I hold the fires passion and the will,
Among the devastation my heart stood still,
The body's inclination ready for the fight,
Statuesque, prepared with all my might,
To break the damn, which blocks the flow,
Quiet nights, the hell I know,
Shared the taste, rum upon your lips,
Questions repeat, lost in the wilderness,
Is love then in vain, who shall bare the cross again?
Wish upon the whisper, stare among the stars,
Should I relinquish hope, tarry off afar?
Picturesque the brush strokes,
Must I pretend, abandoned at the rivers bend,
The painting thus reveals time holds the end…

Author…Dave Lord

Deep inside the darkness. . .

Deep inside the darkness, flickers a light,
Desiring to illuminate,
Though it is covered, by the sins of night,
Greed and lust complicate,
Inquiring how to survive,
Upon this earthly plain,
Knowing, sadly, to stay alive,
Sometimes it's in the game,
Asking forgiveness, while reading the rules,
After the action takes place,
Wanting salvation from other fools,
Feeling inside disgraced,
Wondering still, will the soul be damned, hoping to see heaven,
Worrying, the light is crammed, the hour strikes eleven,
Seeking the word and searching the bible,
Sharing Jesus to start a revival,
But read of hypocrisy, and how the verdict stands,
Confused, as the prophecies, I a simple man,
Ask of the church to save me, they too betray,
On my knees often, questioning, as I pray,
The hour quickly ticking by, midnight soon at hand,
The time of revelation, bestowed upon the land,
Yet by who's adjudication, who dare decide,
For those who judge others, judgment there resides,
The battle inside continues, wanting eternity,
Trusting of the venue, grace upon souls precedes,
For I know I'm a sinner, and of God I believe,
Of good and honest living, I do as I perceive,
Of my understanding I'll hold on to faith,
And at the stroke of midnight,
The light prevails, to show my face...

Author...Dave Lord

Deprived. . .

When one is hungry one eats, when one thirsts they drink,
When one is aroused, they force that feeling in a box and lock it away, Shameful
masturbation shunned and kept at bay,
Leading one to further frustration, sexual deprivation,
As time goes on these needs not met, emotional and physically ill one gets, Mood
swings, tension and violence provoked, simple solution and antidote, Healthy and happy
active couples enjoy sex twice a week,
Marriages are less than half, of those who want to speak,
If you've lost determination, sexual deprivation,
When you find a partner and share a trust,
Explore each others sexual lust,
Find a certain joy which blooms,
Possibly become bride and groom,
Then finances take a toll, a baby is born,
Shifting goals, intimacy is torn,
Less and less remove the clothes, less tingle in the toes,
Soon the neighbor down the street, becomes an inviting treat,
Once across that line, it's just a matter of time, sign the papers,
Absorb in career, share the children, go out for a beer,
Earn more money, trying to survive, another victim of sexually deprived, Another
week, another month, sometimes another year,
Shy from that feeling, because the taste of fear,
Life becomes aggravation, learned the fate of deprivation,
Massage parlors, escorts, strippers rejoice,
Scream to the mountains; let them hear your voice,
No longer is it prostitution, therapists get certification,
Hang the paper on the wall, sexual therapy is the call,
$250.00 an hour, with recognition,
Treating those of sexual deprivation…

Author…Dave Lord

Depth of the Sea. . .

There I see you, all the rage
Beauty, eyes can tell
Hold the heart in the cage
Or else it would wreak Hell
For the heart controls the mind
And the mind controls the page
Your beauty would make blind
A man of certain age
Though I am the younger
Not much more time I have
But yet to be your lover
A soul could be had
So there you stand near me
Where I long to be
If beauty were measured
As the depth of the sea
Then I found the treasure
I would drowned for thee
Take along the journey
Take along the sun
Tell the world to hurry
Life has just begun
You are the obsession
You bring forth the fire
I dream to possess you
My flower of desire
Again to see the tropics
Beneath the waters blue
Again my wish to frolic
When I am with you…

Author…Dave Lord

Destiny. . .

Though life may throw its curves at me,
I will reach my destiny,
There inside the mind is set,
I don't want to know regret,
Everyday at each sunrise,
I see the world inside your eyes,
Happiness I never knew,
Is in my heart because of you,
I may not change the world I see,
I may not cure a sad disease,
I may not find fortune or fame,
Or succeed that well in this life's game,
But survive and know a love that's true,
Destiny, I'm next to you...

Author...Dave Lord

Dimension

A dimension opens in the mind,
A drop of water from the neck drips down the spine,
Leather worn breaks the inner droll,
Lest ye be weary, bless the wooden scroll,
The temperature drops, ice forms on the wings,
Traffic stops, therefore who shall sing,
Trench is dug beyond the bush, dare not we breathe,
Soldiers approach on foot, come dawn, should we squeeze,
Send home what remains inside the box,
Ignore, the floor, where the blood drops,
Once more, implore, coffee on the lips,
It's war, be sure, as the heart skips,
Prepared destiny for the sons and daughters,
Play station, call of duty, have been ordered,
Generations sold out for pieces of silver,
Convert, request, necklace from the jeweler,
'Judas' kisses upon the cheek,
Jesus, betrayal, nations weep…

Author...Dave Lord

Disguise. . .

Take away the wickedness; strip from me the lies,
Have the world unmask itself, removing its disguise,
Follow the tracks of tears, trace the magic high,
All are in the atmosphere, to blind the open mind,
Tumble from the frightened ease, drag the heavy load,
Towards the cold does freeze, scan the bar code,
Enter in the rabbi, son, I will not hide,
Maker of the futures cry, to this I'll not contrive,
Listen to the radio, write the new program,
Direct them on the way to go, acknowledge it's a scam,
Cut the inner lining, empty the pool,
Crack the good books binding, seeker of the fools,
Hold on to forever, today's about to end,
The dates the 12th of never, a dollar for 2 yen,
So tell me what's for dinner, chicken or beef,
Are we not all sinners, why then must we grieve,
Let's drive to the store and buy designer clothes,
The earth we'll just ignore, tie on yellow bows,
Another highway for another mall,
The farm there before, how the corn grew tall,
Over population, older are the aged,
This drugs rejuvenation, class, turn the page,
Collect the homework and pass it to the front,
Neglect the owner, drop back ten and punt,
Brief me on the cases I'm about to try,
Frowns upon the faces, I'm not sure why,
Can you find the answer, somewhere deep inside,
The universal cancer, trapped within disguise…

Author…Dave Lord

Disappointed...

I am disappointed in me
Barely making ends meet
Struggling from week to week
Not holding on financially
Then there are those who ask me why
Tears weld up, inside I cry
But anger explodes from my voice
Especially, when implied, my choice
I didn't ask my first wife to cheat
And tear apart my family
My second marriage found defeat
When my wife sexually would freeze
Then I feel from grace
The guilt I would embrace
Twice my marriage fails
I am left with bills and ails
Now I've turned 50
Can hardly support myself
My daughter, so sweet
Now she tries to help
But I look into her eyes
And inside I can't disguise
There is no more I can do
To help her make it through
I should have my life in order
I can't even help my grand daughter
If my child wants to wed
I've no money I could spend
And marriage number 3
Is not working well for me
My pay keeps me alive
Just enough to survive
My wife, no help from her and
I feel like a burden
I can't start a college fund

57

I feel like my life is done
Attempts to make my mark
Are crushed beneath the dark...

Author...Dave Lord

Distance. . .

In the distance, there I will be
If you feel you will need me
My eyes may not see
My hands may not touch
My ears may not hear
But my love is tough
From a distance I'll be there
Helping, guiding, encouraging
Breathe the air, sense the feelings
Trust your heart, soul be willing
The hardest part when winters chilling
Go forth, insistent
I'll be there, in the distance…

Author…Dave Lord

Distracted. . .

Distracted by the music on the radio,
Listening on my way home,
Look up raise my head,
See the lights, they're all bright red,
Switch my foot, slam on the pedal,
Hear the glass and twisting metal,
God help me, I don't want to die,
On the roof I flip and slide,
Reach in my pocket to get my phone,
There's no answer, no one is home,
Think of my family tears fill my eyes,
As I start to realize, I can't say good-bye,
Spare the truths, forgive the lies,
All I want is to say good-bye,
Made them laugh made them cry,
All I want is to say good-bye,
Shared some secrets some I hide,
All I want is to say good-bye,
My daughters grown, a thank filled sigh,
All I want is to say goodbye,
Where I failed, God knows I tried,
All I want is to say goodbye,
Was my parents joy and pride,
All I want is to say good-bye,
My grand daughter touched the oceans tide,
All I want is to say good-bye,
Though God is calling I guess its time,
I love you all, but I must say goodbye…

Author…Dave Lord

To:

Dollar. . .

It is but a dollar, that shalt not be spared,
For the taste of some, fools would not dare,
Thus, under the sun,
Quaint, the lucky one,
Food he squanders just for a kiss,
Thirst as thunder, he trades for a twist,
A drop of wine for a house to live,
To lick the vine, money he gives,
Home, the earth is a bed,
What food there grows,
A rock for the head,
The thirst is owned, where the dollar is needed,
The sweet shows where plans are seeded,
The future holds what aired maybe,
Justified by lust, not by greed,
Sense the touch and hear the sound,
Lay the beauty on the ground,
Beg another dollar please,
That the thirst be quenched,
Spare the queen, of the common stench,
Which defines the drug affliction?
Love is the addiction…

Author…Dave Lord

Don't miss. . .

Don't miss trying, while searching for yourself,
Don't miss enjoying your good health,
Don't miss your children's youth,
Don't misjudge waiting on the truth,
Don't miss laughter counting your tears,
Don't miss living while hiding in your fears,
Don't miss family reaching for the stars,
Don't miss caring, accept who you are,
Don't miss smiles absorbed in a career,
Don't miss life counting the years,
Don't mislead harming trust,
Don't miss love, time ends soon enough.

Author...Dave Lord

Drenched. . .

Sin drenched pages, strong the undertow,
Check the gages, aircraft flying low,
Read the story; share it with your friends,
Making history, at the rivers bend,
Lie upon the beach, sunscreen on your back,
Hear the sinners preach, server has been hacked,
Breached the security, lock down the doors,
Misused word is **'free'**, finish up the chores,
Sexuality, quiet sex is dirty,
Wash your hands and feet; pray that you are worthy,
In the darkened room, shadows, sounds and moans,
In the interim, thou shalt be alone,
Daydream; fantasize, hands upon the quest,
Inside, memories help with the unrest,
Pay attention to the details,
Intervention, interest starts to fail,
Need the lover, flesh and hair and blood,
Search the covers dare to clean the mud,
Drive to the corner bar, purchase a beer,
Dollars in the fist, the scent of lust is near,
Change the direction, stay on course,
Taste the affection, penetrate the force,
Cake is decorated, hold the icing bag,
Baker you've created, that which you may brag,
Squeeze the frosting and dot the I,
Bring some candy, taste the pizza pie,
Will tomorrow, to shine the sun,
Life is borrowed, glad to have come...

Author, Dean Lord

63

Drown. . .

Life has been a challenge and it continues,
Never know what is next on the menu,
Work to survive, survive for work,
Paycheck to paycheck, tell the clerk,
Can't afford to get a room, another night alone,
Failed the economic boom, buy an iphone,
I understand my father, respect my parents more,
Who then is the judge, forgive the local whore,
For one must choose what's right, and one must beg to eat,
Prepare for the flight, the ticket shows the seat,
Some who hold the money, share a little too,
Thus to let the lonely, pay the bills past due,
Swim among the serpents, down beneath the flies,
Draw the curtain, bury the survived,
The cost of astronomical, there for all to see,
Run toward economical, smile if you please,
There's the empty coffin, close and lock the doors,
More people out of work, finish up your chores,
At a dead end, credit score is low;
No other options, no cash to borrow,
Out there in the water, see the little boy,
His head has gone under, is there any joy,
Slowed is the market, investors somewhat shy,
Trucks deliver goods, still nobody buys,
Shall we crank the wheel, milk is about to turn,
Homeless gets a meal, twelve acres have burned,
Smoke on the ocean, tires in the bay,
Church has devotion's every Sunday,
Saw another mountain; pour a glass of wine,
Drunk fell in the fountain; it's all about to climb,
Prices are the issue, a shiny brand new dime,
Bought a box of tissues, it's ok to cry,
Flowers on the table, diamonds in the ears,
Horse escapes the stable, Wal-mart now owns Sears,
Get a loaf of bread and a pound of butter,
The cashier says, '$20 for you order'

Smell the chicken fry, the shoes are colored brown,
No one has tried, the little boy drowned...
Author...Dave Lord

Dual edged sword

In my hand it felt so good
It empowered my soul
I wondered if I should
Was I ready for this goal?
Knowing each side of the blade could cut
Noting the care I would need
Feeling the nervousness in my gut
But wanting to succeed
It was to soon, my skills not yet ready
My mind jumped ahead
My hands were unsteady
But I mastered the single edge sword
So very well
My experience, I could move forward
The cut, hurt like Hell
As the blade sliced into me
My blood spilled on the floor
My experience not yet worthy
My greed, I wanted more
Now, the wound I bare
Taking so long to heal
Efforts valiant, I unaware
The power of the dual edged steel…

Author
David Lord

Each. . .

Each day you're not near,
My heart breaks more,
Each hour disappears,
Tears upon the floor,
Each moment awake,
Feelings grow stronger,
Time drifts away,
Won't wait any longer,
If I'd leave this earthly shell,
My soul won't be content,
For I'd miss my angel,
To me you're heaven sent,
For happiness to be,
I need you next to me,
Twist, the lemon drips,
Kiss upon your lips,
Sweet the loves taste,
Fear of death fades,
Turn the clocks ahead,
Breach all the rules,
Run to her instead,
Or I would be the fool…

Author…Dave Lord

Each nail. . .

Each nail brings the boards together
Each board becomes the frame
Windows, doors and steps
Trees, shrubs and grass
Workers made all of them mesh
Then, at last you see it
Finished, it's done, your house
Electricians and carpenters
Painters and plumbers
Create this masterpiece
Now it's up to you
To make it complete
Furniture and family
And love, like candy
To sweeten up the place
Add some memories
Then you can embrace
The once house
Which, stood alone
Has now become
Your happy home…

Author
David Lord

68

Emotion. . .

Where is it? Can't feel the emotion,
Stand or sit, I need some devotion,
Please remit is there an expression
Cancel bliss, there's been termination,
Remedy love, in need of protection,
A pound of seed or an ounce of prevention,
Woe is me, my chest knows the tension
Cannot breathe, my lungs fill with congestion,
Can't you see my heart is not pretentious?
Make believe your love is precious,
You can grieve once I'm plantation,
Smell the greed, counted as gracious,
I concede, sell the contagious,
Life's disease is over rated…

Author…Dave Lord

Energy. . .

Mastering the energy deep inside of me,
Hopefully one day, I'll recognize complete,
Fool cut in front of me, wish him dead,
Forgive my anger and the words I said,
Be ye not afraid to close your eyes,
For when you do you reach the other side,
Where is life taking you, how shall we meet?
Praise the one and holy Jew, nails in hands and feet,
Who is of such cruelty, thanking God above,
Civilized society, filled with so much love,
Burn the candle at both ends, working like a dog,
No one appreciates; the rain has brought the fog,
News on the radio, killing everywhere,
Why do you suppose there is so much despair?
Now I have heartburn, taste is in my throat,
Watch what you eat, got to buy a roast,
Morning coffee, at breakfast burnt the toast,
Toys are in the attic, baby clothes too,
Seems there is static, make a pot of stew,
Heading for the shore, like to walk the beach,
Aids, there is no cure, can't understand her speech,
Mountains stand forever, but slowly erode,
Water keeps us living, pave another road,
Those who have the money never let it go,
What is the priority, does anybody know,
Must be entertained, actors on the stage,
Will you sustain, life to turn the page,
Hush, time to watch the show...

Equitable Insanity. . .

Walking on the edge of laughter, waiting for a clue,
Trying to avoid disaster, wondering what to do,
Giving every inch a yard, rent the limousine,
Tell the waiter rolls are hard, restaurant of cuisine,
Damn the pennies, dress the human doll,
Where's the money, I've got to take this call,
Here's the plan
Buy the new mustang, condo on the beach,
Give it all to charity; live out on the street,
Make a million dollars, sink the cannon ball,
Dry the cash by Easter, spend it till next fall,
Lips upon the nipple suck the wooden spoon,
Begging for a nickel, read the bible soon,
Diamonds are forever, coal burns in the stove,
The two are of equal, look there off the cove,
Brother can you help me, need to find a friend,
I'll not quit till Tuesday, she'll love me in the end,
Spare a cup of coffee, mistress will you come,
Naked on the back seat, hear the motors hum,
Equitable insanity, that's where I'm from...

Author...Dave Lord

Eulogy

At my eulogy I wonder what they'll say
He worked hard but little did he gain,
Owned 2 houses, but gave them away,
Married thrice with the third he stayed,
Had 3 churches taught in 2,
Enjoyed poetry and wrote a few,
Enjoyed fishing in his younger years,
Then caught up in his career,
As a dad he did his best,
But now its time he lay to rest,
Won't be forgotten for a while,
Passed on some memories to his child,
Fun and loving, that's a yes,
Often failed to know success,
Wished he'd known financial wealth,
Dreamed to care like no one else,
What he earned he quickly spent,
On the gifts heaven sent,
On children and wives he chose to love,
When times were tough he rose above,
Of all the crutches in life,
Women were his weakest vice,
No booze, no drugs, no cigarettes,
Work, there could be some regrets,
Overall, happy I guess,
Well good night Dave, get some rest…

Author Dave Lord

Ever Always. . .

Ever always searching, still I can not find,
Love beseeching, am I alive,
Heart has cried, soul it bleeds,
Not found the one to fill the needs,
Every pain suffered, every sadness felt,
Has been delivered, has been dealt,
Though I've survived, it's hardened my core,
This hopeless romantic still seeks more,
Electrifying nights, glorious days,
Smiles and a touch like morning suns rays,
Utopia feeling, Lord Let it be,
Fill my eyes with laughter and my heart with song,
Happily ever after, a sense that I belong,
Reach down and bless this broken me,
Loving Lord, I'm begging you, please…

Author…Dave Lord

Fabric . . .

Tearing at the fabric of life,
Cutting into the soul,
Pulling at your heart,
Melting in your mind, a hole,
Ripping at you day and night,
Gripping at your thoughts,
Wondering what it's really like,
Age becomes the cost,
Ever searching,
Always seeking more,
Is it really felt,
Behind heavens door,
Often it is held, but never long enough,
Who are the lucky to truly fall in love?

Author...Dave Lord

Father time. . .

If I could turn back the hands of time
And change my destiny
I'd wrestle father time for eternity
Going back to fix the wrongs
Rewrite the words to my life's song
To sing the way I'd wish to be
My life could be in front of me
With time enough for my daughters play
Cash enough, my bills are paid
To care enough not to stray
Believing God to be the way
Learn to not find fault
Realize I'm not earth's salt
To anger less and not to judge
To laugh more, then to budge
More outdoors, enjoy each day
Not work my life away
Then when time passed with a blink
To life I could turn and wink
Smile and say "I'm all set"
To leave this life without regret...

Author
Dave Lord

Fathers Day

What Father's Day means to me
Getting the tackle for our fishing spree
Load the rods, get in the car
Talk with Dad, the lake was not far
Sit on the bank, ready to fish
It would never end was my wish
Then one night the phone did ring
The message was more than just a sting
Listening, hearing, to what mom said
Tearfully, "Son your Father's dead"
Now, each time on Father's Day
I think of all Dads' special ways
Our fishing trips, our time together
A part of memory to live on forever
So, if you see me by the lake
The tears are just from memory sake
It was not often said, but dad you know
I miss you and love you so.

Author
David Lord

Feel the pain. . .

Can you feel the pain begin?
Close the door and open sin,
Read the words of righteousness,
Entering, allow loves kiss,
Stir the brew of can't resist,
Crumble, beneath the fist,
Turn the knob of emptiness,
Feel the strain and drink the lust,
Pray for those unjust
Hide the unsettled dust,
Climb inside the shattered trust,
Brief the moment unsecured,
Taste the beast, procured,
Blame the curve of timelessness,
Tame the curse of simply blessed...

Author...Dave Lord

Fish. . .

Once upon a time, I'd awaken with a smile,
Looking forward, all the while,
Then life got complicated and paths became frustrated,
Nothing seemed to be the same,
Over obligated, love is over rated, not one for the fame,
Job became unstable, food upon the table, loosing at the game, Overpopulated, time,
something traded, blinked from year to year,
No more elated, thoughts less concentrated, more often wipe a tear,
Birthdays are belated, memories need persuaded, laughter didn't come,
Debt had been created, heart no longer waited,
Soul is empty, where's the fun?
Judgment always stated, undereducated, though money pays for education, Work
the duration, past the coercion, remember words spoke of a reward, Soon the futures
present, no, I don't regret it, but more is never heard,
Blessed that you are eating, not worth repeating, can't afford the bills,
Keep anticipating, the worlds not hesitating; reach for what you will,
Drop the dreams you've painted, fools have nearly fainted,
Cast reality to the wind,
Kiss the one you've hated, hell is often jaded,
Place your hand into the bin,
Time has terminated, cancel and erase, that of what you wish,
Turn the page of shaded, drink the waste you've plated,
Throw your line into the lake and fish…

Author…Dave Lord

Fish and Chips. . .

Here they come, Anne and Pete
Friday night and it is time to eat
Hear the staff announce
"They're so sweet, here every week"
50 years together
Muddled through all of life's weather
Through the good, through the bad
In the happy and the sad
His weak heart her sore hips
But every Friday fish and chips
Out to eat still hand in hand
Holds her seat this gentleman
She kisses his cheek he smiles wide
'That's true love' I heard beside
There was envy some dried their eyes
Those who did, it was known
Tried to disguise but was shown
They wished for love like that
Pete winked at Anne and Anne winked back
Then someone asked, "How'd you do it
50 years of marriage"
Pete answered, "Our love is true and we knew it
When we failed, Jesus carried
You see to commit in marriage there is 3
First there is God, then Anne, then me
When you have the priority straight
You will not fail and life is great"
Thank you Pete, for the tip
Please enjoy your fish and chips…
Author…Dave Lord

Fish Swimming. . .

Fish swimming in the deep blue,
Fish suffering what should they do,
They can't find water no matter how they try,
Wishing, hoping for a miracle,
Wanting to find that drinking well,
Not realizing its water they are in,
Ever drinking while they swim,
Thus are people all over the earth,
Begging pleading for Gods worth,
Where is he, save me, help?
Ever creating their own hell,
Looking for the water they are already in,
Praying for more as they swim,
Whimpering, crying where is God,
Look closer, where is He not,
In the clouds, in the trees, in everyone of you & me,
On the earth in the sky,
And for those of you who imply,
There's no God he can't exist,
In other words you atheists,
You first must believe before you deny,
Suppose the doubt is already applied,
All searching harder and harder,
Excuse me fish, we are in the water,
Sort of like, where is the air, I can not breathe,
Why has God forsaken me?
Just inhale there it is, we are the ones who resist,
And ask when will we prevail,
If you're alive you can't fail, you fail if you don't try,
That won't happen until you die,
So breathe in breathe out and try once more,
The miracles? Look in the mirror

Author...Dave Lord

Foolish. . .

Forgive my foolish ignorance,
I pray my soul be kept,
Each year I learn a little more,
My self is where I'm swept,
Taking a moment to look back over time,
I can't seem to answer the question, why?
I was not around much, always so busy,
Maybe the answer is I'm running from me,
Jobs where I could travel, little time for home,
A bit of time for all, the rest would be my own,
Making plans and dreams, excusing their success,
Blaming the world, for this timelessness,
Buried inside, accept my lies please,
Truth be told, I'm running from me,
Can't bring them back, the moments that I've killed,
I'm sorry for my act and the tears that were spilled,
Now in a rut, the dollar in control,
Another truth or lie, God help this soul,
Where does one turn?
Who holds the key?
Rescue, oh Lord, this soul inside of me
Ready to share the love you have given,
Commitment is the fear, which my heart needs risen,
Offer peace this world can not supply,
Help me forgive the sinner named I,
Turn around the inner self and choose to set it free,
Soon I must stop this running, from that self, me!

Author...Dave Lord

Fools. . .

Fools are they, who disrespect another,
Fools are they, who take advantage,
Fools are they to judge a brother,
Fools lie beneath the branches,
They who walk into the room,
Then seek to pleasure,
They themselves create the gloom,
Passion fails forever,
Fools are they, who spit upon the decent, of a lover,
Love can not feel the touch,
When one holds a cover,
Hands upon the wickedness,
With no one to care,
Pours upon self the sadness of despair,
Choke on their saliva, when they try to kiss,
No term of endearment, healthy love is missed,
Jump upon the willing, who hold gracious there,
Upon the beating heart, brace ones self to share,
For once the love begins, lover please be ware,
The fools shall lack the luster and simply disappear…

Author…Dave Lord

Form. . .

Dreams of hope and prosperity,
Form in a world of uncertainty,
The rules applied from yesterday,
Have all since gone away,
Hard work and promotions once could fill the void,
Loyalty and devotion are now what to avoid,
A business fails a new one arrives,
Laid - off trying to survive,
Every job needs an education,
To wipe your nose you need certification,
When did we all get so terrified?
You see the fear in everyone's eyes,
If you hold a job you feel lucky to work,
But the pay applied makes you go berserk,
Prices everywhere on the rise, taxes to increase,
Paychecks no surprise, raises have now ceased,
A tank of fuel for your car will cost you 50 bucks,
Food to eat and rent to pay, extra well good luck,
Loaning money from the bank institution,
Well it's easier to pass a bill in the constitution,
How can one progress, it's an act of Congress,
So we walk upon pins and needles, waiting for the next evil,

Author...Dave Lord

Forest. . .

Do you see the tree there in the forest?

Of which do you speak, can you point to it,

The one with the leaves there under the sky,

They all have their leaves it is summertime,

The acorn lies beneath, it is a mighty oak,

There are many, which do you see,

That one of which I spoke,

Since there are many and you speak of one, be more specific,

There, under the sun,

Why do you try me, please touch its branch,
Ah, the one with the broken limb, the bark falling to its side,
The one that may not live but probably will die,

How could you decide this when from a distance you couldn't see?
The one different of the many,
Judge not, what you can't see from afar,
The weakest of the weak can turn into a star,
Judge not the forest judge not the trees,
Help them move forward, thus helping you and helping me…

Author…Dave Lord

84

Fragile. . .

Life, fragile as a crystal goblet,
Though taken for granted,
Running for an outlet,
To escape emotional bandits,
Move past pain and follow through,
Missing the point of what one could do,
Not for self, not for glory,
You won't be remembered past the story,
Laugh each morning, be thankful to awaken,
Take time with friends and family, before life is taken,
Anger, please put it aside, and ignore that sense of pride,
Place your fears on hold, love like Jesus told,
Patient and kind, forgiving and blind,
Open your arms for a hug, open the mouth less,
Ignorance learned is the drug, of the opinionated guess,
Suffer not the children, blessings to one and all,
Prayers for the fallen, gracious God hear the call,
Each breath inhale deeply, each tear wipe away,
Each smile made widely, each and every day,
No not for the money, for it does grow on trees,
As the paper it's printed, both will burn with ease,
And of the things they borrow, materialistic guy,
Are held until tomorrow, grasp not on the lie,
Greed is the obsession, working for the cause,
Egos determination, weakens flesh to loss,
Thus of possessions, just meet the needs,
Share without question, for others human deed,
Then with eyes glaring, then with heart free,
There might be more caring, a changed philosophy,
There might be more caring, a changed philosophy...

Author...Dave Lord

Freeway. . .

Headed down the freeway, towards Virginia Beach,
With the top down, this car is a beauty,
You in your bikini, I in my swim trunks,
Lust surfaces between us, like we 2 were drunk,
Hold on to the shifter, keeping it in drive,
Car is moving quicker, please enjoy the ride,
Pistons thrusting, hope to spare the rod,
Water dripping, underneath the bod,
Back off the pedal, engines getting hot,
We can hear the sizzle, the radiator pops,
Sprays on the hood, coolant everywhere,
Though I'm not sure I should, it's as if I don't care,
I drive into the tunnel, without antifreeze,
Hoping that the engine won't decide to cease,
Moving slower, hear the tires screech,
Passing through the Chesapeake,
On the other side, insert the hose,
Filling up as needed, time to change roads,
Pull into the driveway, park the garage,
Once we check in, the day is a mirage,
Pushed against the head rest, pull on the hand brake,
Reach between the seats, feel the car shake,
Shutting down the motor, letting her calm,
I like the way she purrs, my little cherry bomb...

Author...Dave Lord

Go ahead and hate your neighbor,
Go ahead, cheat a friend, do it in the name of heaven,
You could justify in the end, there won't be trumpets blowing,
On that judgment day, the bloody morning after,
The tin shoulder drives away,

Between the shadows of yesterday,
Between the shadows of fear,

Dig for gold, change the oil, time to catch the train,
Its all mine, dinner time, wash behind your ears,
At the mall, at the beach, music of today,
Alarm yells, go to hell, drink another beer,
Mistaken steps I've taken are just your opinion,
Life unappreciated, love becomes stagnant,
Hate anticipated, arguing over fragments,
The most important job is picking up the garbage,
Take your medication, try to relax, breathe in the filthy air,
Antiviruses, spam, update security,
Absorb the news, be like him, cameras follow her, everything compare,
Tickets to Disney, accept the blues, join the gym, color your hair,
Too much debt, financial aid, spend more money,
Stocks are down, closing bell, help the economy,
Commercial, ads on the radio, what's the sell,
Send a donation; use your credit card,
Big brother is watching, says you are speeding, a ticket from a photo, Everyone's broke,
restaurants are closing, there's no place to go,
Smoke your cigarette; it makes you look cool,
Lung cancer, you're the fool, sue the company,
It's your choice; they're to blame, responsibility,
Smoke your joint, medicinal purpose, won't be legalized, ten years the same,
Broken hand, skinny man, cars are driving fast,
Newspaper stand, farmers land, time to kill the calf,
Swim the river, eat your liver, can you cut the grass?
Paint the house, kiss your spouse, and pour the turpentine,

Draw a bath, kick his ass, drink a glass of wine,
Orange juice, chocolate moose, change the flat tire,

Dreams fade, hide away, sing in the choir,
Schools, institutions, educate,
Cruel, prostitution, inmate,

Between the shadows of yesterday
Between the shadows of fear,

Go ahead and help your neighbor
Go ahead and greet a friend,
All in the name of Jesus
Purified in the end
When the trumpets blow on judgment day
The glorious morning after
On his shoulders, through the gates…

Author…Dave Lord

God. . .

God, still searching…who am I?
Some think I'm this wonderful guy
But within I'm reaching for my place to be
Inside tormented, where is me?
Looking for love to touch my soul
Wanting to give it equally so
Yet, finding pieces without completion
The puzzle forms, but parts are missing
When will I find him, where is your plan?
I've looked deep inside me…who is this man?
Soon may he rise up and find a way out
I pray and I wish, except I have doubts
Grasping for something I'm not sure what
Help me seek him, my savior, His blood
So that I may know, who this man can be
Help me Jesus, to find me…

Author
David Lord

Grandpa's car

I over heard a young girl say
I'm going to my Grandpa's tomorrow
He said I could have his Hyundai
To keep not just to borrow
I smiled as I listened to the details she did share
"A 94, equipped with power windows and air
Then I went back in time
There thoughts went through my mind
"My Grandpa said the other day
I could have his 53 Chevrolet
Vinyl seats, 3 speed, AM radio
But I'd need to work out more
Before I could drive it though"
Cause the standard steering is tough
And I'd have to be strong enough
And I'd need to learn the clutch
And remember it idles rough
I suppose some things change for the better
But Grandpas sharing their old cars
Makes them greater…

Author
Dave Lord

Grass. . .

Select the color of green,
Read the lines in between,
When it rains stand and dance,
The veggies need the water,
Fill with wine and tip the glass,
Go in line and place the order,
Lay your lover on the grass,
Under the moon, complete the task,
Clean the drippings from the pan,
Brush the dirt off your pants,
Walk the beach, feel the sand,
Pair of peaches with a tan,
Have a favor in deep to ask,
Keep the stem within your grasp,
Turn around enjoy the treat,
Paddle across the stream,
Pull the shorts down off the line,
Baby slow down, take your time,
Blow the bubble till it pops,
Get to loud they'll call the cops,
Drink the milkshake through the straw,
Swing the bat and catch the ball,
Play the game of newlywed,
Drift away to face the dread,
When will your buns need toasted,
The coffee beans are roasted,
Take breakfast in the bed,
Pull the sheets over your head,
When awake take time to spread,
The peanut butter on the bread,
One more time before you go,
Plant the tree so it may grow...

Author...Dave Lord

Grave. . .

Watched the sunrise, danced among the fools,
Listened to life described, by all the schools,
Followed my career, I'm on my fourth one,
Joined the church, believe in the son,
Drank some whiskey, drank some wine,
To my baby, sang a lullaby,
Worked my hours, earned my pay,
Spent it all on yesterday,
Wished on hope, hoped on high,
Occasionally, some tears I'd cry,
Traveled by boat and by plane,
Stood under the sky in the midst of rain,
Only part of life I've missed,
In an angels arms and kissed,
Though I've searched, though I've tried,
All the love did not survive,
If I were to coin a phrase,
Happiness is in the grave…

Author…Dave Lord

Grown. . .

"Get them to grow up and get them out"
That was what we joked about
But now that there are boxes packed
There's more to it, that's a fact
As the tears stream down my face
As the emptiness fills this place
The truck outside waits for the bed
Realization in my head
No more toys to move aside
No runny nose I need to wipe
No skinned knees I have to bandage
Just pack the clothes and the baggage
I smile and act all tough
So she won't see me crying,
She thinks I'm rough
So that's the act I'm trying
Still, deep down my heartbreaks
Another step in life to take
Both for my daughter and me
She's all grown up, now set her free…

Author
Dave Lord

Hair. . .

Hairs flowing down her back, her eyes touch the soul,
Treasure beauty graced, worth a vault of gold,
Breathless as the body speaks, check the pulse behold,
Endless sensual sweet, breaks the heart of cold,
Skin, precious to the sight, trust weakened, request the bold,
Lust breaks into the night, desires about to unfold,
Loveliness tells the fright, wait not on hold,
Place the hand upon the centerpiece, both ready to dine,
Tables carry the feast, arch the crooked vine,
Shake the whipped cream; spray some in the mouth,
Heard are the screams, delight spoken aloud,
Thankfully appreciate the exquisite taste,
Gently kiss the cheek of this angels face…

Author…Dave Lord

Eyes. . .

I saw the hour glass upon the table,
The sand was partially gone,
I wondered if life was able,
To give love equally strong,
Realizing half my time had passed,
Many memories have been daunting,
Reflected in the looking glass,
There the future is haunting,
Anticipating the journey,
So I look to escape, once upon a time,
Beauty there creates, since, you I find,
Shadows of forever, share sight with me
Happiness I've never, felt nor conceived,
Dim, the lighting reveals, emphasized,
There I see tomorrow in your eyes,
Voices of the choir echo from the halls,
Thoughts of dire, disappear in the walls,
Once there before, sensations come to call,
Placed by the door, touch the fireball,
The candle is still burning,
Fixated on the notion, whether it's truth or lie,
Aiming for emotion, will not criticize,
All is devotion, lover do not cry,
Teardrops are unwelcome…in your eyes…
Teardrops are unwelcome…in your eyes…

Author…Dave Lord

Hear the quiet. . .

Hear the quiet
Deafening sound
Even my heart
Fails to pound
Waiting, wanting to hold you
Begging, hoping soon
She'll be near me
Her lips touching mine
Her breath on my neck
Her smell on my mind
Her arms squeeze me
Her voice in my ear
It's so lonely
When you're not here
Forever, since you've gone
Anticipates the dawn
Each day passing
Each night, as well
How long to suffer
This painful hell…

Author
Dave Lord

Heart of Gold . . .

Heart of gold, Heart of mine
Often sold, Often blind
Taking chances, make a wish
Seek romance, Pain, to which
Sometimes felt, sometimes given
Often melts, Romantic living
Be more careful, be more wise
Search more graceful, Watch for lies
Sometimes felt, sometimes given
Often melts, Romantic living
Heart of gold, Heart of mine
Less often sold, sees more, I find
Takes less chances, less often wishes
The romances, have been switched
Into neutral, not in drive
Much less fruitful, am I alive?
Heart so cold, Heart defined
Takes no chances, does not wish
Fears romances, makes conditions
Excuses galore, Provides a safety
Chance no more, less pain…I'm hoping…

Author…David Lord

Here today. . .

Here today, start the year, numbing of the mind,
Carry the cross, plant it there, just beneath the lines,
Attach the wires, telephone, cable, electric,
Pull toward the house shell, there to be connected,
Felt inside the summers breeze, heard the voices echoing,
Life and family, begins the metamorphoses,
Trickle down the spine an endless chill,
Protect the inner child, overkill,
Blend a side of rudeness, with a cup of 'me',
Add a pinch of arrogance, stir it carefully,
Turn the oven on, turn up the heat,
Bake the chiffon, crack two eggs and beat,
Appetite requesting, try another meat,
Always ever tasting the same side of beef,
Something's in the water, boil before you drink,
The sewer is backing up, can't you smell the stink?
Time to call the plumber, cat has run away,
Dogs are always humping the neighbor's new stray,
Pay the bills, buy the groceries, need to fill the tank,
Gas again is rising, make the pancakes,
Mistakes we are making, stress from the job,
Drinks you are taking, dress like a slob,
Go out to dinner, remove the trash,
Can't afford the mattress, pocket full of cash,
Children off to college, life just past on by,
Look to what is left, call legal advice,
Time to start over, nothing more to share,
Chop up some clover, nothing to compare,
Back at the apartment, sip a cup of tea,
Tenderize the chicken, rub on the bay leaves,
Ready to go out and paint the town red,
After the news, to late, gone to bed…

Author….Dave Lord

History. . .

Another second ticks, then ticks away,
History in the making each moment of each day,
While life passes, on this time machine,
This planet holds on to every destiny,
Changing direction, clouds and wind,
History starts when the day begins,
What will be done with this historic time?
Reputation, feel alive,
I'm growing tired and realize,
History is made; I stare at my own eyes,
What mark is left behind, a child of mine,
Souls I've touched, some passion some pain,
For a moment, then refrain,
Mystery lives, review,
Bare my soul, you look right through,
Beat the drum of righteousness,
Buy another round,
Sense the rush, make another sound,
The dark now covering, breathe an empty sigh,
Once more, summary, day is passing by,
Abhor, make believe, that I could stain the sky,
Another day tragically, burns into the night…

Author…Dave Lord

Heart and Soul. . .

Hit and run, heart and soul,
Steal the riches from the old,
They're not well in their mind,
Take their cash, thief in the night,
Hit and run, heart and soul,
Speak of love while lust enrolled,
Seek the treasure touch the gold,
Once for pleasure, grieve what's sold,
Heart and soul, hit and run, expectations overdone,
Manipulate words of thought, experience, life is taught,
Heart and soul, hit and run, one more drink, one more drug,
Relationship has been reached, cheating heart and soul impeached,
Hit and run, heart and soul, abusiveness, there left a hole,
Lack of feeling, lack of faith, hurt is etched upon the face,
Hit and run, heart and soul, emptiness the shell erodes,
Love is missing, tear filled lies, and bend your knees to justify,
Hit and run, heart and soul, buys a gun to overthrow,
Finds no peace, the truth is blind, heart and soul prepare to die…

Author…Dave Lord

Hot. . .

Hot summer evening, condo at the beach,
Standing on the patio, trying to catch a breeze,
Cold beverage in your hand,
Behind you, your loving man,
Brushes the hair from your neck,
You feel his tender kiss,
Slips your dress to the deck,
And says "we won't need this",
Quiet fills the sigh, hand upon the breast,
Gently touch the thigh, on the bed you rest,
Lips on lips, warmth to increase,
Arch the hips come with a scream,
Ease the strength between the moistened place,
Slowly accepting all the length,
Silhouettes merge into the dark,
Rhythmic pace kept with the heart,
Senses lost into delight,
Breathless, most of the night,
Sweat pouring onto the sheets,
Love soaring soul's inner peace,
Lying together lust not needed,
Her in his arms thankfully greeted,
Together stare at the stars,
Wonderful happiness right where you are,
Saved by the dream I can't achieve,
Wanting a wish to believe,
Simply described as what I see,
Time for sin with you and me…

Author…Dave Lord

How. . .

How shall I deny, the teardrops in my eye,
Love again I try, once more it is good bye,
Dream the lover true, lost the love from you,
Life no longer tarries, when the lover marries,
Damn the passions sultry, damn the morning sky,
Now charged with adultery, stand upon the lies,
Wicked are the feelings, blessings have arrived,
Sickened now are healing, cross to bare then die,
Blood drips from the fingers, erase the fantasy,
Flies upon the trigger, fire if you please,
Heart no longer beating, curse the seven seas,
While the curtains blowing from the evening breeze,
Hand upon the shovel, plans are buried there,
Pin to burst the bubble, father do you care?
Sink the navy vessel; make a pot of tea,
Platoon is in trouble, kneel, its time to grieve,
Who can sense the warmth when it's cold outside?
Where does one go just to take a ride?
Child are you praying, ask the universe,
Crumble up the painting, trash, its equal worth,
Drink then of the fountain, hold on to your youth,
Praise the Virgin Mary; define for me the truth,
Stale is the bread, grow another seed,
Taste the bullets lead, penetrate the need,
Forget all the tomorrows, waste not alive,
Fill the tub with sorrow, another chance to cry...

Author...Dave Lord

102

I am Sorry Father!

I am sorry Father where I have failed
More often then not my sins prevailed
Constantly begging to be financially free
Often filled with pride or worry
Forgetting I'm nothing more than dust
Giving into my weakness, lust
Wishing for more than I need
Being ungrateful when I succeed
Comparing to others more wealthy than I
Turning my back and closing my eyes
To helping those less fortunate
Gripping tightly to the mighty buck
Asking forgiveness to what I won't forget
Forgetting to forgive and then regret
Hurting others for my own selfishness
Not completing my own forgiveness
Only being thankful for your graciousness
Angered when life falls short of bliss
Not reading the word continuously
Not falling upon bended knee
Looking for more then enough to live
Precious Jesus, can you forgive?
Help this soul to a better me
To serve you for your glory
Allow this heart to share the message
So others will find the saviors passage
From sin and shame to heavens gain
From sin and shame to heavens gain…

Author…Dave Lord

Recall. . .

I recall a time you held me with respect,
Now I wonder, in your mind is there regret,
Concerned, are there lies upon your lips,
Recognize, as passion seems to slip,
Less often under star lit skies,
Do we sweat the night away?
Request, dignify, where we are today,
Hide not the truths within your heart,
Curious, for once I touched the mark,
Share, whose light forms the colors of the prism,
My fear to learn, alone is my prison,
I seek the fire in your eyes,
Its shadow wears a dark disguise,
Loved once where the fires glow,
Trusted there beneath the rose,
Knowledge, I breathe, I sigh,
Gently slice my love good-bye…

Author…Dave Lord

Illusion. . .

What is life but ticks upon the clock,
The calendars pages turn,
A house of wood and block,
The moon and sun burn,
Day in day out drive to a job,
Ten hours for a wage, some time to sleep,
Sometimes to live, a little left to play,
Then the hours shift, responsibility,
Try to balance work, career, and family,
Decades come and go; your life becomes a blur,
Then wake to find, nothing has occurred,
What you thought you knew, and who you've claimed to be,
Nothing is the truth; your life's a mystery,
Laid off from that job, no money for the bills,
Learn a new career; take your tension pills,
A test that needs passed, or soon out the door,
Now you push a broom at the local store,
One point in your life earning 60 grand,
Now 8 bucks an hour, you feel less of a man,
Wife looks at you different, fights have gotten worse,
Stealing 50 cents, from your daughters purse,
Bank account is empty, bills are piling up,
Sense your marriage ending; life is in a rut,
Move back to your parents, ex-wife gets the keys,
The house, the car, support, and alimony,
Look into the mirror, just turned 43,
Parents getting on you, you drink excessively,
Inside your mind, troubled by confusion,
How the hell did life, come to this conclusion,
Come to realize, its part of the illusion…

Author…Dave Lord

Incompetence. . .

We've bitten down hard upon the bullet,
While they've amputated our wallet,
Now sitting the chore, as we watch, incompetence,
Government spending, trillions in debt, yet they tell us not to fret,
Magicians with mirrors and smoke, I'm not sure but I think we're all broke,
I've heard the news, I've done the math, and though I'm no accountant,
The numbers I've added shows to me, more incompetence,
Billions thrown at AIG, Fannie Mae, and Freddie Mac,
$700 billion stimulus when Lehman's fell flat,
A second near trillion dollar stimulus, billions on these wars,
3 trillion owed to China, need I say more,
Bailing out the banks, GM and Chrysler,
Cash for clunkers, housing help, California fires,
Bush left office with $13trillion of debt,
Obama spending more, incompetence,
'**But**' the recession is over, fix health benefits,
Send more troops, who's our economist?
We have yet to stop counting the unemployed,
They too get government funding; I'm getting annoyed,
How much money will we spend, will we ever see black again,
Swimming in a sea of red, passed to our great grand children,
This isn't right it isn't fair; it can't be true no one cares,
There must be something we can do, let us not let our greed shine through,
Let's place a salary cap on what we can make,
$5 million a year is enough for goodness sake,
Everything more is then placed into the pot,
All the extra money will help, would it not? This could cause prices to drop,
Take baseball, $10 million a year to swing a bat, $5 million with the salary cap
Now cut in half the cost of a seat, then your credit card won't feel the heat,
CEOs and Dr's do the same, Athletes and actors all those of fame,
A million here a billion there, the deficit less difficult to bear,
And billionaires consider this trend; give it all back except 10 %,
Help the politicians gain some confidence,
And rid our government of this incompetence.

Author…Dave Lord

Independence. . .

Fall to sleep in a dream, hope filled tapestry,
Hanging from the walls in the mind, could they ever be,
Ease of heart that love exists, life engulfed with smiles,
Free to feel the graciousness, happiness of a child,
Color, play, fantasy, stress relief of heavenly,
Closely look upon the wall, answers in the tapestry,
Drive to a casino town, play the bet and lay it down,
Numbers on the wheel display, head for Independence Day,
Hopes and dreams and wishes voiced,
Are now in reach, just a choice,
To tell the tales evermore, are in the hands,
There before, for in the world of human greed,
Though difficult the destiny, in the hand,
One does hold, a ticket worth a pound of gold,
Thus a beach house of envy, and a limousine,
Diamonds and the beauty, blessed to hold the key,
The promises foretold, no longer shall they lie,
New cars and trips, behold, are gifts before one dies,
Birthdays some were missing, anniversaries too,
Are cared for from a distance, all are overdue,
Proudly pass the blessing love should be shared,
The heart now sends the message, the soul it always cared,
Now family and friends, kids and lovers too,
Stand upon the ship, a toast before the cruise,
Champagne in the glass, feast soon begins,
Lips upon the flask, sails now full of winds,
Words are spoken just before the sip; belief in life was woken,
Then the glass tips, the heart in love found true,
Reason for believing, to reach then I knew,
This dream was worth achieving...

Author...Dave Lord

Innocent

I held my daughter, age of one,
Loved her the best that I knew,
Though work was calling, had to run,
To provide a house and food,
Taught her what I learned over these many years,
When her daughter was born,
My cheek was filled with tears,
For I understood then the meaning of innocent,
I among my glory fell to the intent,
Of the world, warn what I should fear,
Learn the education, taught with heart felt sneer,
For once like the virgin, we smiled happily,
Then came the knowledge of "supposed to be",
Crush imagination, trust reality,
What is real, save what we believe,
With determination forward same as we,
Tomorrow's are forever, lest one should die,
'Read what I teach, stare not upon the sky,
Follow not a dream but do the same as I',
Behind the mask one wears, you'll find the tears they cry,
Who then can be innocent, when passed on is sin,
The only days of innocent, are when life begins…

Author…Dave Lord

Intimacy. . .

Though protected, dare to make a wish,
Greedily I call, before the tools tarnish,
Push the fork into the tender meat,
Utilize the utensils, until they become weak,
Take upon the hammer; thrust it to the floor,
Snug the tongue into the groove, hesitate some more,
Nail it in place, apply the stain,
Excess on the face, wipe away,
Fit the pipe inside the other, may the waters flow,
Seal the leaks, in turn discover, pipes expand and grow,
Place the plug into the outlet, careful of the sparks,
Electric juices going, sometimes cause an arc,
Insert the pencil to the sharpener soon becomes the point,
Write, the lead softens, sharpener repeat,
Hasten the insanity, may it ever be,
For the other side of sanity,
Standing there is me...

Author...Dave Lord

It Is. . .

It is your war not mine,
With time, comes a fragment where which I forget,
The years of two have approached,
And they also have come to pass,
Sin brings forth the wicked, not of my control,
Yet by yours have these things been,
Be not with a lover, take up your cross and cry,
Blessed are the few, not the many,
Live among the swine,
Bare false witness, be ye the judge,
I've become the target,
The linen upon the bed is soaked,
Shattered has become the glass,
Lost there in the thicket, branch before thy scroll,
Of family I know not your kin,
Who am I, not your brother?
There beneath the watchful eyes,
Of food, oh Lord, be there plenty,
Chaos and trouble bind, thou goals have much regret,
The hand upon the engines stroke, speak to those of your past,
Step not on the cricket, a battle will unfold,
Brace the walls, collapsing from within,
Lies tell to your mother, put aside peace before you try,
There before you find the penny,
What are the thoughts inside your mind?
Your house of cards block the sunset,
The hopes held go up in smoke,
Life now becomes the simplest task, once more to fill the basket,
Knead the dough and sense the droll, feed the multitude,
Break the bread, begin, who goes there?
Trust falls asunder, hate, henceforth to die...

Author...Dave Lord

Jump . . .

Jump into the water, outside the tires screech,
Pastor at the altar, remote is out of reach,
Enter subtle complexity, never again simplicity,
River trickling towards the stream, feed the worm a centipede,
When will life become crazy, never knew the voice of reasoning,
Sun upon the pumpkin seed, corn and wheat,
The bread is stale; we're out of meat,
Toilets overflowing, children are all growing,
Click the mouse to send, welcome to the world of pretend,
Virtual reality, anything you want to be,
Bring back the sanity, left lane closed in half a mile,
Throw on a side of beef, daughters pregnant with her first child,
Meet me at the restaurant; I hear that you're a grandparent,
Back to work retirees, fight the war in Istanbul,
That thing is incredible, could you please pass the salt,
Need to find a masonry, dog is getting spayed and fleas,
I can't believe I just ran out of gas,
Where's my glasses I can't see,
Animosity, 40th anniversary,
Grandpa what career shall I choose,
Bank lean on the property, letter in the mail,
Foreclose on the company, could someone post my bail?
Got to buy the groceries, oceans trashed with mans debris,
Postman shot outside the mall, at the job interview,
Excuse me while I take this call, what's the importance,
Robbers in the house, red car passing,
Are we all to blind to see, life is all about conceit,
Like some antipasto? Enjoy your movie,
Popcorn please, jumbo,
Extra butter, watch your cholesterol,
'Drink, I'll have bottled water,'
Australia is down under,
Yes it's somewhat comical, what our thoughts perceive

Author...Dave Lord

Just. . .

I would trade it all, just to be,
Care not for the sympathy,
Illuminate the inner peace,
Bring inside the fantasy,
Holding on too, what is free?
Curse the destiny, summer night by the sea,
Shelter ones own family,
Work the hours to drink or eat,
Candles light the darkened street,
Build your bridge across the bay,
Clouds cover a sunny day,
Rain upon the emptiness,
Fill the shame with bitterness,
Reaching for a pint of bliss,
Drunk again and have to piss,
Sell the broken mule,
To buy a piece of glass, money, smile fool,
The future is now past,
Simple, can't you see, you're not allowed to pass,
Hear the old man wheezing, smoke a cigarette,
Seems in life, struggles what we get,
Chances that we take, failures what we make,
It's all the grand design, suffering in ones mind,
Tell yourself you'll get there, dance among the thieves,
Wealth is in despair, lost in disbelief,
Raise your weapon soldier, aim and shoot to kill,
His father stands before, rifle fires with a shrill,
Tears fall onto the dust,
Climb aboard the battleship, USS trust,
Where all shall follow for they must,
There, one can be, just...

Author...Dave Lord

Justified insanity. . .

Justified insanity, ignorant integrity,
Found among the multitudes, senseless distant gratitude,
Excellence fades into gray, will, is lost to attitude,
Belief is no longer gauged; touch the selfish plague upon the earth,
Hell cuts in its own rebirth, crass individuality,
Bursting at the seams, sloth dedicates itself to the scheme,
Underlying arrogance, tells of the expectancy,
Dull the mind of eagerness, fill the bowl with emptiness,
Confused by the smiles disagreed, please the mediocrity,
Cheat the laborious casualties, agitated by the obvious greed,
See the structure start to sway, notice, placed upon the dread,
Age is nearly halfway dead, clench to ones desires,
Build an open pit to hold the fires,
Welcome, 'come what may', jealousy broadens below the stone,
Break open the urgency, escalate the energy,
Notify the clergy, trust is to be left alone,
When shall bliss enter the unknown?
Child is your supper getting cold? content is the tambourine,
Listen to its jingling, aggravated there before the throne,
Negotiate, for all is gold, pampered are the emperors own,
Delve into the entity, Christ's love shalt ever be,
His blood drips upon those, disregard authority,
Avoid responsibility, able bodies cast your broken bones,
Cease the military, kill those who won't think like we,
Sirens silently tone, thoughts of a disaster,
Slave becomes the master, savage universal plea,
Farmers pray before they plant the seeds,
Call upon your pastor; speak the words of intricacy,
Give thanks before you eat...

Author: Dave Lord

113

Kissed. . .

Kissed the angel of death,
Brushed against its wings,
Twist, sensed the knifes edge,
Fate trades, chill brings,
Smell the stench of greed,
As the sparrow sings,
Cut the mouth it bleeds,
Wasp, feel the sting,
Shift flames burst,
A moment to breathe,
Passed the black hearse,
Awaken from asleep,
Tell the tale of escape,
Thankful on thy knees,
Lips will ever taste,
Chance once more believe,
Strike the livid serpent,
Desire, the soul's disease,
Saved, the angel circumvent,
Set the wicked free,
Life the happy hour,
Death the endless nap,
In thy grasp a flower,
Sounding of the taps,
Stand against the tree,
Shaded from the sun,
Hear afar, the eulogy,
Released, the grave opens…

Author…Dave Lord

Last Day. . .

This day may be the last upon the earth,
But life each minute I know its worth,
Each smile, each tear, each person I met,
Each love, each fear, each moment of regret,
Each hug, each kiss, memories I'll not forget,
Each child, each heart this world my touch would let,
Each friend, each family member gets,
To carry on the dawns a gamblers bet,
And each time you remember me,
My soul is made whole, in heaven graciously

Author...Dave Lord

Lay me down…
Lay me down close my eyes,
Deep inside, my soul it cries,
Broken heart in my hand,
Another day sorrow expands,
Not a prophet or a saint,
Try to breathe lest I faint,
Overwhelmed by life it seems,
Not prepared, expectancies,
House, family, provisions needed,
Goals reached but gold exceeded,
Hear the knock, the doorbell rings,
Bill collectors with warnings,
Mortgage due, cupboards bare,
Bellies empty, standing there,
I have tried; I've not cheated,
Yet at fail I have succeeded,
My children look beyond a stare,
The pain I feel beyond compare,
Done all I can and some more,
Looked to God, knees on the floor,
Need a job, want to work, believed if I would assert,
All could be as I dreamed, another lie another scheme,
The truth, if stockholders sell, plants close, 'to bad, oh well',
The rich stay rich, their wealth exceeds,
The working stiff gets cut and bleeds,
Unemployed, government expense, further, economic tense,
As the days number by and my will to survive,
Gun in hand I turn to crime, wealthy man keep your dime,
Convenience store, a 100 bucks, hear the sound, lead in my gut,
God I'm sorry, I truly tried,
Lay me down, close my eyes…

Author…Dave Lord

116

Life. . .

Life has a beginning life has an end,
The time in between with family and friends,
Make up the story of who we become,
The smiles the tears the laughter and fun,
Blessed upon the earth for the time we live,
Touched upon our hearts the love we give,
Share the memories from our minds,
Promote what we've learned,
See the hopeful treasures,
Reach the dreams we yearn,
Graciously wrap our arms around the soul's request,
Pleased, God lays us down and calls us home to rest...

Author...Dave Lord

Light...

Light breaks through my window of a brand new day
Get my shower and get on my way
Another 12 hours worked for 8 hours pay
Evening falls, the sky turns to gray

Light screams in to open my eyes
The TV sounds some words to the wise
Shuffle my feet into bed
To rest for another day of dread

Light flashes and sirens blare,
The reflection in the window shows I have less hair
The ambulance attendant states we're almost there

Light crashes in, as the doctor exclaims
'The procedure was successful, do you feel any pain?'
My chest is sore, but I am okay

Light flickers on, what is this room
Unrecognized this smell of gloom
The clock shows it's almost noon
'Time for your meds and a walk outside'
I try to stand up I'm barely alive

Light dimming, where am I now?
Though I see myself I am looking down
Airflows over me like a wave
A tombstone, I see my grave

Light cracks, dawn of a day about to spread
The world continues...but I am dead...

Author...Dave Lord

Molly...

I laid my head upon the grass
And looked into the clouds
I saw a girl in a frilly dress
Laugh and dance around
Her eyes sparkled as sunlight touched her cheeks
Her hands reaching, she shook the nearest tree
Birds flew all around, seems they too could see
This beautiful little girl, her name Molly
I saw as she smiled and crinkled up her nose
Her smile creates a dimple, she has 10 little toes
Happily she played there, I could feel the breeze
As I lay watching, joyfully
The sun began to settle behind the clouds of gray
Molly waved 'good-bye' as she skipped along her way
She reached her hand towards heaven, and there I could see
A hand grasped hers and put my heart at ease
God was caring for her, which comes as no surprise
But if I ever wonder, I'll stare into the skies
I'll not forget the blessings, which came to be
The love, the heart, the soul, of an angel...Molly

Author...Dave Lord

119

Loaded Gun. . .

The entire world fighting for freedoms
Yet by who's design?
Better off, when you have the gold
Then this freedom is defined
'We won't be undersold'
Yet we sell out just the same
Do what we are told
Who is running this demented domain?
Educate to a higher degree
Get a job and earn money
Follow the rules of the conspiracy
You're free to purchase, what you need
As long as the profits will proceed
Then the stockholders and business succeed
If all these things do not align
Out on the street is where you'll find
When success fails you will see
It's not about you; it's not about me
It's all about wealth it's all about greed
All the games and all the fun
Will stare down the barrel of a loaded gun…

Author…Dave Lord

120

Hold On. . .

Hold on to my heart, for the time we are together,
Keep it safe in this dark, a feeling, I wish ever,
But I know when you depart, returns the alone,
No fires will I start, soon I'm back too on my own,
Fear and anxiety, I face the stormy weather,
Sadness and empty, I'll know this painful tremor,
Why then do I try, repeat this endeavor,
To self I can't deny, the existence of the pleasure,
Is there hope upon this earth, for a love to stand forever?
As to one a new rebirth, which contains a wealth of treasure,
For I've tried and yet I fail, where is my happy ending,
Every chance a fairy tale, guess that chapter is still pending,
Hold on to my heart, and please don't let go,
It could shatter into pieces, don't you know,
Would it matter, there below, why my lovers have lied so,
Take tomorrow from today, sell the soul its natures way,
Where is hope upon this life, who does send the candles light?
Hold on to my heart; bring the sweet and gentle part,
Die alone here on the mark, never more desire sparks,
Here inside this broken heart, here inside this broken heart...

Author...Dave Lord

Sigh. . .

Another day reaching through, another pulled away,
Though patience is the virtue, it doesn't ease the pain,
More time must erase, before I know bliss,
The hours chase, the moment missed,
The stone falls from the mountain, the lining has a rip,
Alone the days I'm counting, to have to make the trip,
Somewhere in the jungle, hear the lions roar,
As the weeds tumble, as the eagle soars,
Triumph over evil, mighty hand of God,
Read there in the bible, in the book of Psalms,
Oceans hold the fish; trees grow towards the sky,
Why then does my wish, always seem to die,
Drown there in the puddle, sent by angels' tears,
Can you sense the trouble, can a deaf man hear,
Emotions become paralyzed, someday please justify,
There before the alter, lay the sacrifice,
Gun pulled from the holster, shoots at paradise,
Homeless woman begs, just that she may eat,
Break a dozen eggs; fry a pound of meat,
Balance the future, the past has gone,
Presently the loser, I will travel on...

Author...Dave Lord

Simple minds

Simple minds there within, deep beside apostrophe,
Intellect, how have you been, see the hidden trophy,
Look into the blackened hole, visualize the opposite of
Droll, stimulate the senses, not the economy,
Rejuvenate tomorrow's possibilities,
Drag the river bed, find the bodies,
Hat placed on the head, do you know karate?
Poke the third eye, that should keep it shut,
Purchase the tuna; it's your turn to putt,
Golf, eighteen holes, drive the balls hard,
What a swing, hit it 50 yards,
Glance upon the watch tower, the numbers do not match,
Lunch is about to start, what's today's catch,
Welcome everyone, to the seminar,
Bagels on the table, jelly's in the jar,
Think for yourself, find the missing key,
Can someone help, that's an oldie,
Song on the radio…purpose, where did you go?
You must get a job; let's turn on the game,
What's the score Bob, nothing is the same,
Simplify the antidote, isn't that a crane,
Go on smoke your dope; the world should be ashamed,
Who are the heroes, will you spare a dime,
Homeless person, should they be alive,
Just align the cross hairs, aim at your target,
Could we see the race cars, let's go to the market,
Shouldn't we know how to grow our own food?
Plant it in the ground that's all you do,
Ask the farmer he'll reply, make a U turn, thanks, good buy,
Bought a pound of gold for a thousand bucks,
How'd you get them all into your truck?

Gone to New York City, got to ride the train,
At the motel going to check in, grab $20 at the ATM,

Simple minds awaken, thus to take the blame,
Of one faith, of one God, it's a mystery,
Don't eat paste, catch the frog, its all history,
Notice the age of those still doing the work,
Did time get froze, or is this bezerk,
Won't you push the throttle, care to debate?
Hand me the bottle, in a drunken state,
I'll handle my own affairs, Grand Rapids please,
Would someone explain why we lend from the Chinese?
The greatest power, soon to be determined,
Borrow one more dollar, was Hitler German,
Stand above the innocence, if they only knew,
There before the monument, double crossed, acute...

Author...Dave Lord

Lonely. . .

How does one begin, listen to the hum,
Pour another whiskey, drink until you're numb,
Who wants to hear of this conundrum?
Deep into the pits of dark, stare upon the pendulum,
Pitch the roof with tar, straight the crooked path,
Ease the spinning mind, drink another glass,
Eclipse the sun and moon, stand on father time,
Inhale the perfumes; bless the holy water, reckless on the road,
Find your happy place, wrap around a smile,
Flip another quarter, spit in the commode, sinister disgrace,
Throw it on the pile, waiting on the slaughter,
While the world is shaking, let the heart be still,
Blood upon the altar, sense your mind is breaking,
Crush the empty will, lull anticipating,
Beliefs push in a jar, while the crust is baking,
Damn, the whiskey spills, thus complicating,
Stare at the ceiling, piss on the walls,
Take another pill, cast another stone,
Love is not revealing, slam the fist and crawl,
Again I am surrounded, again I am alone,
Tear begins to weld, wipe and clench my teeth,
Curse the day to hell; black my soul and feet,
Always stand erect heard in monotone,
So with self respect, trust the creaking bones,
Conjure up conviction pay another bill, break open a bottle,
Fire up the grill, rush inside the possibility,
Tell the world conclusive, anxious iniquity
Life, once again, lonely…

Author…Dave Lord

Longevity...

It seems love doesn't have a guarantee
It feels like life is never simply
Two people holding on to longevity
Once a woman falls for a man
And that man asks for her hand
All the things which brought them together
Is the hail that forms the stormy weather
And you'll find there will never be...longevity
Sure the years may come and go
But the sweet love fails to show
And as time pushes on
The love they had once, now is gone
The hearts slow their beat, no longevity
As the bags are packed, the judge sets custody
The children learn to love differently
And fail to love just like we
The thing which suffers most, longevity
So how much time must tick away
Who wants to wait for loves company
Who cares about longevity?
The foolish romantic...ME...

Author...Dave Lord

Love Inside. . .

I found love inside a bottle, her name is brandy,
She won't ask much, but sure tries to please,
Just open the cork and pour, sip to let her in,
And if you want more, there's no arguing,
I found love inside a pill, which takes away the pain,
The high is such a thrill; I can't find much to complain,
I found love inside a book, black letters on the page,
The promise if I look reveals I will never age,
I found love on the internet; I can have without regret,
No room for jealousy, I choose them on my screen,
I found love in an empty place, all alone I can not face,
Is there one who even cares, take a seat, but there's no chair,
I found love inside music, turn it loud to confuse it,
The sound is uncontrolled; will it touch me to the soul?
I found love inside a jar, as I eat it in my car,
I enjoy this endless feast, now my bodies is obese,
I found love in a woman too, but that love seems to be untrue,
Happiness won't come through, divorce is harmful too,
I can't ever find this love; I've looked low and high above,
And the hurt is not worth, the lose is so much worse,
I found love inside myself; it's a love like nothing else,
Not conceit, its deeper still, and a love that can and will,
Survive eternity; throw away the earthly things,
Like the world, it's large enough, to release the finer stuff,
Then when love is in need, I can share for I indeed,
Learned love can never be, till I learn to love me…

Author…Dave Lord

$\mathcal{LLS}$ . . .

Love lust sexuality,
Dove dust sensuality,
Sex trust complexity,
Words must sensitivity,
Door bust infidelity,
Age rust longevity,
Unjust society,
Time was energy,
Life curse generally,
Wish plus money,
Woods bush consistency,
Local push politically,
Need tush constantly,
Job rush terminally,
Dream crush disbelief,
Tomorrow lush luxury,
Doubted much therapy,
Don't fuss life complete…

Author…Dave Lord

Love Starved. . .

Starved for love, love starved,
Searching at the local bar,
Looking for someone to meet the need,
The heart wants fulfilled, lust, the in between,
Accepting less each moment, reflecting ever still,
Time is the component, the mirror shows the ill,
Drink the vodka tonic, to reduce the pain,
Relationship platonic, failed at love again,
Step inside the dark room, and then adjust the eyes,
Heart relives the sad gloom, who shall criticize,
Empty the emotions, enter sex refined,
Sink into devotion, just to feel alive,
Losers become winners, take the morning pills,
Accept another sinner, just to pay the bills,
Find a lover; he must be the one,
Disappears from you, how old is your son?
Holding back the sadness, holding back the tears,
Another day's false gladness, another glass of beer,
Take one more tug, let the lover in,
Waiting for a hug, tears upon your chin,
Break another promise, break another plea,
To self you vomit, again you disagree,
Plan the wedding, take the vow,
Hell becomes the setting, life left its frown,
Who is able, define love for me,
See the stable, Jesus set me free,
How a sinner wills to want to be,
Eat your dinner the belly you must feed,
In the dumpster, trash becomes the wealth,
Sell the toaster, chocolate starts to melt,
Sweltering summer, winter brings the snow,
Accept the beating, dance one more show,
Believe that mistrust is reality,
Another starved for love, just like me
Author…Dave Lord

129

Loyalty

Whatever happened to loyalty?
Was it lost in the 60s?
Attitudes formed since 1955,
All for one, to self survive,
There under the judgment tree,
Just inside the military,
Brother to brother has no qualms,
Not since before Vietnam,
Forward now, come what may,
Below the sky of somewhat gray,
Brotherhood of loyalty, honor and integrity,
Seems to have drifted aside,
The other choice, accept the bribe,
Not for others, not for life,
Not for lover, to hell with pride,
Selfishness, it's a pity,
No self respect, no dignity,
Won't accept authority,
Slash the throat of loyalty,
Kick the balls of honesty,
Spit upon the choice of free,
Based upon stupidity,
Watch out for the double cross,
Take in stride the enemy,
We are all expendable, count as loss,
It's all about the money...

Author...Dave Lord

Lust. . .

Cold day, crisp night, logs upon the fire
Chardonnay, candlelight, passions desire
Hands touch, lips kiss, love inspired
To much, linguist, lustier
She hears the words spoken
Clothes fall from her back
Senses and emotion
Fill the room of black
Musk from the bodies flow
Skin upon skin
Held by the candles glow
When is it sin?
Lovers share their lust
Dreams form in the dust
As the day returns
Morning sunshine burns
Eyes are opened, satisfied
Off to work, a long good-bye
Sensual thoughts, passions true
Soon to be home again with you
Timeless moon and sun
Another day begun
Off they fly, wave of hand
Less they form the sounding band
Countless hours collectively
Elsewhere their spirits wish to be
Another heat, another soul
Beating heart, they want to go
Lust, temptation gone
Anxious for the dawn
At a lovers new found lair
Hours now dwelling there

Back to house, responsibilities
Lust and love form this disease

Togetherness, a hard swallow
Seems like Hell often follows
End the game and close the book
Heaven cease from a new look
Away towards the ocean floor
Lust, not found anymore
Slain in the deep of night
Alone and peaceful, troubled sight
The wish once held the sweet grown trust
Settled there beneath the brush
Accompanied by the dead of lust
The heart and soul are less defined
And life again has flat lined…

Author…Dave Lord

Man. . .

Man is made for joy and woe,
Some born for sweet delight,
Twisting toward the blackened hole,
Some born for endless nights,
Some to win and dance, some to lose and curse,
Try, they to advance, destiny before the Hurst,
Stand upon the mountain top and scream 'I am here',
The world deaf from inner thoughts ignore the thunderous cheer,
Where is the escape from this misery?
Paging through the book of mystery,
Lust the anathema, weep on life's web, bound are the desires,
Lost with self esteem, the thread within the briers,
Honey sweetly pours, forgive the butchers knife,
Quickly towards the door, shed this dreadful life,
The soul wears the hat of dunce, harlots were virgins once,
Beauty for a bit of bread, the flower held beneath the dread,
In the mist I cannot flee, laughs heard from the crowd,
In my prison I am free, wearer of the crown,
A fiber from the brain does tear, challenging, does one dare?
Upon the stool warmed from the chill, and by comes an angel,
Songs from the cherubim, rung like church bells,
Doubt, self contradiction, silence fell, across the room,
Sensually grant decision, love told with truths intent,
Defeat the lies sin invents, if protected from on high,
A nation, one can sell or buy,
A child's toy and an old mans reasons,
Are the fruit for all the seasons,
Thus in love time crossed, before love was lost,
In the heart hear the cries; a mother hums a lullaby,

Once was love, sadly dies,
Released, the moment ripe, fallen and left go,
The pain, as a strip, the tears from lovers flow,
Oceans roll and drown, aged ignorance, profound,
Why do priests promote the wars, while soldiers kill for peace?
Anger then becomes the chore, of all who are deceased,
Therefore, nations near or far, blessings to all of you,
For right there where you are, God is there too.

Author...Dave Lord

Man of war

I stand here in Afghanistan I just turned 20
I'm barely just a man, this my reality,
Is this Malthusian, what do they want from me?
Weapons in my grip, and strapped upon my back,
Food, clothes, an extra clip, and my nap sack,
Sent me for the other man, he is of evil,
Crouch and with my trigger hand,
Aim and shoot to kill,
The sound of the rifle echoes in my ears,
Recoil on my shoulder brings my eye to tear,
'Yes, it was a hit', I see his flesh explode,
Blood I see it drip, upon my boots toe,
He upon his back lifeless with a thud,
'My God upon my hands I wear another's blood',
But what has he done me; believe what is the lie,
I invaded his home, death; you hear its cries,
I find it hard to breathe; I guess it's from the guilt,
I look down to my chest,
I see the blood that's spilled,
"Why am I here" I fall to my knees,
"I wish to go home to my family",
"What is happening", blurred is my sight,
'My God, why was I sent here to die'?

Author…Dave Lord

Management. . .

Worked my way to management,
To earn a better wage,
More responsibilities, all comes with age,
Work more hours in the night, scheduling the days,
More stress, my chest is tight, can't give out a raise,
Disgruntled employees, attitudes are bad,
Lay-off notice handed me that I get to pass,
The news to those now out of work,
This part I know, they'll consider me the jerk,
Performance low, the ax they hand to me,
They hide inside their office, the president and VP,
Mark and Molly, Steve and Joe, I'm the one to let them go,
Sad inside but they don't see, they'll just think 'hypocrisy',
"He said when he'd get this promotion; we would not need worry,
So, is this what he means, glad the event worthy",
Going home in misery, my stomach tied in knots,
Knowing I have to sleep, but I won't get a lot,
Toss and turn, I start to sweat,
What could I do, I am such a wreck,
Tomorrow I'll spread the work,
Those left must do more,
This is quite degrading, I understand the whore,
Do what you do just to get that buck,
Turn and walk away, wish them good luck,
Can not think about what just occurred,
Lack of conscious, like a lawyer,
And daily the lies from a Doctor,
Telling someone they'll be cured,
When the truth, they're unsure,
Yet, on this day I respect them all the more...

Author...Dave Lord

Miles. . .

Mile after mile cutting through the night,
Counting the markers with my headlights,
Follow the blacktop under my wheels,
Stare at the clock, eating my meals,
Exit by exit the years passing by,
'It's a living' convincing, I try,
White lines painted, I'm hypnotized,
Brake lights flashing, emphasize,
Slowing for one more delay,
My home life seems so vague,
The hours I work, I'm hardly there,
My pay frozen the cupboard is bare,
Eventually I get back to the house,
A moment to share with my spouse,
Off to bed a few hours of sleep,
Alarm clock sounds, time to repeat,
Burning the hours brings sanity,
Believing the lies I often keep,
'This is how I earn my money',
Yet fears of a net of safety,
There is the truth, the reality,
Still, for the moment it works for me,
Success, what I'm hoping to reach,
To the eyes of society, whatever that might be,
Praying I won't die, while I'm seeking the need...

Author Dave Lord...

Miracle. . .

Enter in the darkened room, now to set the stage,
Endless night, over soon, turn another page,
Lust is in the senses, too collect the pay,
Though the hearts intent, bold becomes the wage,
Light as the candle, illuminates the stars,
Back upon the table, Rush…there you are,
Part of the miracle together there in Love,
Treated as imperial, collect the ancient drug,
Wrap around the pole, taste of citrus wine,
Penetrate the droll, deep within the mind,
Excite the emptiness, treasure quiet still,
Just another part of the miracle,
Blood of the lifeless, nearer to the hand,
Gently feel the brush, of the sinful man,
Entice the inner self to breed the distant sun,
Colors of the prism, circles everyone,
Mystic is the background, song begins to play,
Heat pours from the dance, where the bodies lay,
Justice, crimes, rebuilt is the temple,
Awakened by the signs, of the miracle…

Author…Dave Lord

Missing. . .

I take a breath, yet something's missing
I see the sky, the darkness kissing
I feel the wind, but there's no whistling
I close my eyes but I'm not sleeping
I wish the wish, yet it's not keeping
I play the songs; still I'm not listening
I wonder long, but there's no inquiring
It seems I'm here, though am I existing
I try to think there is no sensing
I speculate, what could this life bring?
Without love I suppose it's nothing
I searched the search and what I'm finding
Is all my mind is rectifying
Day and night my spirit's blinding
From my heart the beat is dying
The only choice that is worth trying
To life itself, the chance I'm taking
Succeeds this soul towards the living…

Author…Dave Lord

Moment

In a moment a New Year,
Trace upon my cheek, the tears,
Another dream another wish,
Fail to succeed instead diminish,
Into a whisper unto the sky,
The dream and the wish say good bye,
Age trickles in, love and life,
Fade again, almost, not quite,
Hope lingers and helps to breed,
One more possibility,
The heart somber, simply weak,
Yet the soul reminds, gesture welcomed, is the reply,
Another minute, another dance,
The willed component, a second chance,
Sun upon the mountain, dew upon the glass,
Distant sound, breeze through the grass,
Inclement weather, knock upon the screen,
Enjoy the view of summers green,
Sigh of relief, see the candles glow,
Flannel sheets, winter winds blow,
The scarf is scarlet, the eyes show,
Believe the harlot, the bible knows,
Chance of a lifetime, in a life, time to chance,
Reflect from the window, another glance,
Begin today, tomorrow is gone, factor in the eclipse,
Come what may, carry on, reserve to take the trip…

Author…Dave Lord

140

Money. . .

Money, nothing more than a purchasing tool
But most of us, not unlike the fool
We see what we want and buy it quick
For that moment of happy, we need our fix
Then to find the next item to fill the pit
And all the while it's on credit
Gaining interest for the lending group
While the borrower slowly drowns in the soup
Not worrying of the consequence
Until the paychecks can't meet the expense
Suddenly looking for a second job
Feels like you're getting robbed
Never enough to pay the bills
Good enough is all you feel
Month to month you make ends meet
'It has been some time, how about a treat'
Out for dinner enjoy the meal
$100 evening such a steal
For the owner of the credit card bill
20% interest should make your bones chill
It is time to think like those in the past
Buy what you need and make it last
Buy nothing more than equals your cash
Credit cards should go in the trash
In time the payments for those debts
'Paid in full' the letter you'll get
Continue that payment into a savings account
Soon you will have some extra cash around…

Author Preston!

Moon. . .

Full moon shining bright, there before my eyes,
In the distance darkened stormy skies,
Angrily they swallow it, lightening strikes the ground,
Ever getting closer, hear the thunderous sounds,
Airplane crosses in the midst, the worlds about to turn,
Diamond bracelet on her wrist, episode of how we learn,
Would thou once play for me, a golden opportunity,
Drain the pasta in a bowl; add the sauce and mix,
Wait to long the pastas cold, conjure up a fix,
Open the photo album, thanks for the memories,
Hear the motors hum, drifting out to sea,
There is an officer of the law, in an unmarked car,
White truck passing, sirens, ah, justice, there you are,
Rain is falling, keeping us dry,
Trains are hauling, a bottle of rye,
Trade inside democracy, trance the mediocrity,
Another day another dollar, adjust the priests upturned collar,
Hence the plastic spoon, once upon a crescent moon,
Younger generation, found at the clubs, future of the nation,
Where to find the love, please modify the budget,
Can of pork and beans, now, who holds the grudge,
Bless you when you sneeze, talk is never empty,
Quiet afternoon, driving in my Chevy,
By the light of the silvery moon...

Author...Dave Lord

No More. . .

No more I wish to pain,
No longer want to cry,
Relationships remain,
No more care to try,
Father, life has ended,
Marriage 3,2,1, rejected,
Son, mother be as it may,
Dad, daughter will for today,
But as the chameleon simply fade,
Into the woodwork hide away,
Lust, when the need,
Will purchase it, respectfully,
Though fear to sin against the throne,
Pray forgiveness can be known,
Once held love like a sand filled fist,
Which sifted through the tight clenched grip,
Made mistakes like many do,
Search more love, no thanks, I'm through,
Bit the apple several times,
Ate the worm trapped inside,
No more will to taste the sloe,
Better off to leave alone,
Better off to leave alone…

Author…Dave Lord

Now. . .

Now that I have touched my dream,
Now that I've felt extreme,
Now that I hold ecstasy,
I awake and you're next to me,

Evermore I'll never grieve,
Earth enables heavenly,
Angels cast down graciously,
I awake and you're next to me,

Hearts can feel the gentle breeze,
Love and life, the 2 shall meet,
Soul filled light in harmony,
I awake and you're next to me,

May the sunshine warm the heart
May the moon beams be a part
Hear the cherubs play the harp,
I awake and you're next to me,

Brush my hand that I believe,
Turn my sadness to happy,
Darkness tossed into the sea,
I awake and you're next to me,

Dear Lord I pray to thee,
Let the sinners sin go free,
Heart and soul shall ever be,
I awake and you're next to me...

Author...Dave Lord

144

Numbers. . .

There is life, numbers on paper,
Terrified, complete total stranger,
Years pass by, dodging the reaper,
Tears I cry, as the numbers are clearer,
Sacrificed, to the worlds parking meter,
Testified, hold up to the keeper,
To self I hide, to step up and greet her,
Crucified, my Lord and my savior,
Justified, the soul can't evade more,
Sanctified, the ways of behavior,
Brutalized, by earth's carnal nature,
Staring back, the edge of disaster,
Empty stack, from all of my labor,
There is no lack, of sharpening the razor,
Feel the smack, counting the treasure,
Red to black, I've not had the pleasure,
Still there's a fact, printed on the papers,
They won't attract, there are no redeemers,
The face is slapped, by the selfish receivers,
Not from a knack, I'm compelled to savor,
Still looking back, there are the numbers,
Just a crack, above a survivor,
Guess I've slacked of being a saver, sad retract,
The time is always moving faster,
Yet, the check book shows, a buck and a quarter,
The check book shows a buck and a quarter...

Author...Dave Lord

Of. . .

Of intellect, are we?
Or, opinions of ourselves...
Of love could we? None yet I've seen,
Provision is not love but living,
Controlling another is selfishness,
Servant to a King does not impress upon one power,
Nor does faith make one to believe,
Yet to believe, thus we have faith,
Happiness makes the soul to laugh,
Fear will make it cry,
Weakness, when to ones self they don't deny,
You wish to own the riches of life,
You pray to hold the truths,
Then put away your money, look towards the youth,
There inside is innocence,
There you find trust, be gentle and forgiving,
Ever thankful, be not threatened by the colors,
But the finest breads, bake,
Most precious is water,
May it be pure and blessed,
Cleanse the guilt with the flood,
Oceans are of these, plant the seeds of righteousness,
Give more than you take, stretch out your arms to hug,
Feel free to help someone, care for the elderly,
Smile as if you've meant too,
But most of all... just be you...

Author...Dave Lord

Old. . .

What have I done for my country?
Was I a good dad?
Am I a selfish freak?
Why is my heart so sad?
I thought people liked me,
Love once I had,
Maybe I mistreat,
And make others feel bad,
I wasn't there often for my friends,
Couldn't be there for family,
To busy working to meet the ends,
Hiding from my beliefs,
Those taught to me from others,
Parents, teachers, grandmother,
What are the thoughts of my own?
I just want to be left alone,
Am I a maverick who doesn't care?
My look in the mirror turns to a stare,
A tug on my pant leg, "Poppy please play"
Words from my grand daughter, she starts to beg,
"No sweetie not today"
I pick her up, in my arms I hold,
"I'm sorry dear, but I grow old"…

Author…Dave Lord

One. . .

One so beautiful, it's hard to comprehend
Dreams unpredictable, though my heart pretends
I wake, your body next to me, an angel sent
We both shuffle to work await the days end
So slowly the day drifts on, I am anxious again
When night falls we are home in the den
Drinks in our hands, invite over some friends
Dinner out, then to a club
Dance the night, and then home for a rub
You lying there as I massage your thighs
You fall asleep with your deep heavy sighs
My arms around you, the night fades
My hope, to always be this way
Day breaks with cloudy skies
I know your thoughts, as I look in your eyes
Soon you are naked to my surprise
A day for love making, I realize
Exhausted, I am soaking wet
Lying in a pool of my own sweat
As I watch you exit, it is well defined
This, another fantasy in my mind…

Author…Dave Lord

Opinion. . .

Pop, pop, pop…heard in the distance from the shooting range,
Didn't stop its persistence, feeling somewhat strange,
Wars fought over seas, Iraq, Afghanistan,
So why is the military target practicing,
Emergency on the radio, I now understand,
Planes overhead, the flag from Iran, we are under attack, trust is broken,
Who is the enemy; watch your back, soldiers flood the streets,
May I volunteer; I am willing to start a new career,
Hell has spoken, protect us naval fleet,
Try to disappear, tanks roll, people scatter, aircraft overhead,
Bombs drop, subject matter, on the ground our dead,
Countless bodies fall unto the sound,
Trying to take cover, bullets all around,
Freedom fighters under siege…We are the good guys, aren't we?

You decide what is real, not I, there underneath the crimson sky,
Into the ocean there to spew, humanities constant brew,
Pollute the water and the air, a dollar's worth is all we care,
Who are you, not like we, submit to our society,
Welcome those which will play, the others, well, they shall pay,
Gas is in short supply, oil prices on the rise…Have you seen, Dubai?
Terrorists have started this; angry men, clench your fists,
Reason with intelligence; listen when you hear the news,
Find within there are some clues, react to what you choose,
Once upon a time, this King, upon his throne to us he'd sing,
Pay the price or fear the cost, righteousness has been lost,
A tax upon your tea…Cast it now, into the sea,
'Well, this is now and that was then, those patriots were minutemen',
Thus, these freedoms we now hold, as long as we do what we're told,
Sad that those towers fell, someone must pay for this hell,
How wise to patiently wait, till pilots they'd be,
Then why fly into those towers so early?
Hmm…miscalculation, honestly, some think to lessen casualties,
100,000 workers there at 9:05, 20 minutes sooner, 4000 lost their lives

Did you know they were built in 1976?
Back then you could use asbestos,
The cost of removal would be outrageous,
The other plane which hit the Pentagon,
Circled 3 times then hit dead on,
To the area of construction,
More lives were spared, another missed deduction,
I suppose, that's fair, the plane which crashed in the field,
That destiny may never be revealed, remember JFK?
What more need I say, Lee Harvey Oswald, you think that's it?
Ok, Chappaquiddick…Abraham Lincoln, set them free,
John Wilkes Booth, civil war, slavery, misconstrue,
Trust the government; you must believe…No, there is no conspiracy,
Where did that notion come from, recall project 51?
Why do 24 hour convenience stores, have a lock upon their door?
Microwaves fill the sky, don't you worry you won't die,
Baked potato, or brown rice place it in, then press 9,
We, the lower class are kept at arms length, lest we spread our disease,
Control them through the banks, which weakens their knees,
If they stand to fight, give them a reward, soon they're out of site,
Sold, they drop their sword, how is it we do not know?
It's been given to us long ago, 3 rings in the circus,
You can't watch all the show; you'll miss some and need to return,
Thank you Mr. Barnum, slight of hand, taste of honey,
Come on back and spend more money,
Somewhere deep inside, someplace, between the lies,
The true color of their eyes, beneath the thin disguise,
Justice there you will find, right before you loose your mind…

Author…Dave Lord

Paradise. . .

Close them; close your eyes and dream of paradise,
What do you see there in your mind, what can you concise?
Feel the warm ocean breeze, white sand upon your feet,
In your hands a martini, sun turns up the heat,
Grapes, cheese, caviar, champagne on the side,
Ocean waves touch your toes, is this paradise?
Go ahead close your eyes, dream of paradise,
Home by the fireplace, snow and cold outside,
Sitting on your sofa, enjoying some food,
With your children lying there next to you,
I'm sure this too could be a paradise?
Once more close your eyes dream of paradise,
Abandoned car, doors unlocked, soft place to sleep,
Thankfully, your children too, can curl up on a seat,
A blanket found in the trash to warm them just right,
A passer by with a meal, a beautiful sight,
A cup filled with change, alive one more night,
Go on; close them, what's your paradise?

Author...Dave Lord

Parenting...

Maybe I'm the one who doesn't belong
Maybe my up bringing was wrong
Maybe I was the one deprived
But here I am and I survived
You see my parents taught me differently
They instilled responsibility
We had stuff, did things, and traveled, though
Sometimes parenting means no
No, you can't have the truck you want
No, we can't afford it
We'll go to the playground and have fun
That's free, we won't need credit
It's ok to go picnic,
Or play catch with that baseball
Your child won't die because you didn't 'buy it'
Whatever 'it' is called...
Sometimes vacations aren't at the Ritz
Whether it be in the mountains or beach
There are ways to afford it
Rent a cabin, buy food for the week
Don't need amusement rides, mini golf is cheap
Play in the sand, ride the waves
And the times you didn't eat out, money saved
Go and have an ice cream
Involve your kids in a hobby
Not an X box or a Wii
But flying a kite or building a model
A Lionel train or a dollhouse
Put it together frame by frame
Build a rocket or airplane
And with an allowance they can earn
The twist, they'll get to learn
So have fun, set limits, and share life's teachings
There you have it...Parenting...

Author...Dave Lord

Path. . .

The path of distant memories,
Feel the pain of the disease,
Freedoms past unlocks the door,
Hide behind the world obscure
Trying to avoid the rain,
Upon the cups brim stained,
Can't run from what darkness brings,
In the night the phone rings,
Rips you from the claws of fate,
Wonder how the soul relates,
Across the bow you feel the breeze,
Destination, make believe,
Dreams inside like cancers grow,
Heat won't let the cool winds blow,
Sweat from a snow filled sky,
Falls upon the long good bye,
Pour the whiskey on your skin,
Let out the sinner deep within,
Snap the whip unlatch the gate,
Summer will no longer wait,
Stretch forth and touch the world,
Before the bell sounds,
Bend and grip the pearl,
There beneath the frown,
Forget to laugh but not to smile,
Tomorrow's empty glass, walk down the isle,
Plans for sorrow, land upon the grass…

Author…Dave Lord

153

Paths. . .

The path is filled with rocks
But you have shoes upon your feet,
The night is bitter cold, but your home holds the heat,
Sin, the righteous stalk, hear the preacher preach,
Laws are ever lawful, until securities breached,
Freedoms are still free, if you pay the cost,
Sheep are endlessly, becoming the lost,
Who will house the thief, no one seems to care,
A stranger takes his seat, the congregation stares,
Who then shall be saved, those of membership?
Until the altar calls, others seem to slip,
Just another number in the database,
Everything is real, accept the liars face,
If the code is hacked, identity is changed,
The thief becomes the prince; the prince becomes the slave,
The homeless beg for food, enraged you turn your back,
You earn a wage, worried insomniac,
For what makes you react, to the sight you see,
Frightened by the hell of 'that could be me',
Selfishly remark, the pain is given,
The homeless still hungry; you apologize, expecting heaven,
Blood upon the collar, death upon the hands,
Spit upon the dollar, cries the wicked man,
He, who steals, to feed his family, kills to save another,
Runs from the enemy, the police officer,
Tears upon the cheek, where did she go wrong,
The mother of the child, who doesn't belong,
In the mind you've done your best,
Worked ten hours, babysitter did the rest,
Not your fault, the world is to blame;
But the hate is equally the same,

When the sunsets, when the day begins,
Which will be the loser, which one will win?
Happy ever after, based on your decision
As the story goes, depends on your religion
Crush the ego, curse the rules,
Change the knowledge, more money for the schools,
The stores are filled with what the body needs,
Yet, the unknown, will you succeed?
Keep the cycle turning, shadow of the day,
One more life's journey, sweep away,
As long as you escaped, you can where the smile,
Swearing at God, to save the next child...

Author...Dave Lord

Peak...

I'm at the peak of life, the pinnacle of existence
Each day of the fight, I become less resistant
Some days I may win, others are a loss
What little I gain, just doubles in cost
Working hard and trying, just to pay the bills
Slowly I'm dying, stress becomes the ill
Hoping, wishing, praying for that miracle
Time is just escaping, debts are several
Get my pay I'm smiling; now I can relax
Write the checks I'm sighing, because there's no more cash
Wait two weeks to get another pay
Repeat the above, it's always the same
Another year ending another round is fought
I feel my back bending; relief is all that's sought
Seems I'm ever spending, to quit is my thought
Life is sad depending, on pay checks from the boss
Just a number to the company
A brick in the wall of society
All in all, under some tax ID
Until your assets gone, then a liability
Even 30 years of honest loyalty
You're dropped like a bag of sheets to laundry
Just a soul survivor, all we'll ever be…

Author...Dave Lord

People. . .

People walk with their eyes closed bumping into things
When they do they open them and still they do not see
Like car companies crying poverty from what the economy brings
And all the crap the government speaks we are to believe
But I need to ask a question or two
Like isn't the Chevy Colorado an Isuzu?
And doesn't Suzuki work with Saturn?
GM with Toyota, Ford with Nissan
Like the Vibe and Matrix without the emblems
Could you pick which was which, one from the other?
So what is all this stuff they are selling us, brother?
And why won't Senators step in
When all the industry goes to Beijing
Hanes closing 6 plants, Chrysler and Hershey
Our jobs displaced at China's mercy
When did America turn into a wuss?
Though we flex to the world, Iraq we push
How many years will this war be fought?
How much of Iraq's land have we bought?
Of this war look at its hell
Billions in cost, so many lives fell
Medical benefits many can't afford
Again, the factories went abroad
Millionaires making millions, billionaires wanting more
While we're serving chicken and scrubbing the floors
Men in there 40's made $50 grand
Now make 7 bucks to empty trashcans

I am not disrespecting these positions
Though when they were opportunities
You could make the decision

Not wake with the thought of serving refried beans
So come on America write your congress
Let's find new ways to clean up this mess

Bring the troops home where they belong
Rebuild America and make it strong
Devote to buy American when at the store
Yes, I understand it may cost a bit more
But tomorrow's lay-off you want to be sure
The job which is lost won't be yours…

M I A 4 A…
(Made In America 4 Americans)

Author…Dave Lord

Perfection. . .

Perfection is more a dream than a reality,
Temptations, we see in fantasy,
The tube we stare and sit,
Life should be like this,
A house, a car, a family,
Everything works and all are happy,
The truth beneath the lies,
There's more than what it seems,
Broken hearts and failures hide,
Underneath the dreams,
Though we trust leaders, on them we believe,
Feel disappointment when they've deceived,
Real perfection is found with Him,
Be a slave to the master, you begin,
Deal with each disaster floating with the wind,
Don't submit to outside interferes,
Never quit, persevere,
Ever trudge through the storm,
The other side your heart will warm,
View the future with candlelight,
Behind the clouds the sun burns bright,
Another tomorrow waits against today,
Slow they may prosper,
Don't throw your dreams away...

Author...Dave Lord

Perfume

The perfume you where is intoxicating,
It fills the air provocatively,
The scent so exhilarating,
One knows perpetuity,
Like she who where's it, perpetual motion,
Ever lasting sensuality, my heart knows the commotion,
A soul deserving regal, my wallet running thin,
Un-righteous is this hell, unjust, there is no sin,
Blanket on the table, bedspread on the floor,
Entice my love unstable, there is room for more,
Breathless is the kingdom, send the knights to war,
When the battle ceases, tunnels to explore,
Push inside the swords blade, deep within its sheath,
The bell sounds for the French maid, bow before the Queen,
Love until the morning, shower, cleanse the doom,
Such an interruption, inhale the perfume…

Author…Dave Lord

Poor. . .

Have been poor a million times,
At the door rang the chimes,
It's the core of bad design,
Carry on and let it shine,
Not a whore, not unkind,
So much more intensified
Blink the dust from the eyes,
Drink the lust of what it buys,
Think once before you hide,
Witness, do not testify,
Take the chances of a fly,
Land upon the apple pie,
Dress the clown walk on by,
Do not sin until you die,
Break the sound and let it be,
Rapture is a travesty,
Will to live set it free,
Alternative, below 6 feet,
Search for good in every soul,
There is wood and there is coal,
Understood the darkened hole,
Light of heaven there within,
Just in time to see them win,
Test the waters before you dive,
Like yourself, while you're alive...

Author...Dave Lord

Punishment. . .

On the other side of punishment, I hope are brighter days,
Foolish decisions were mine to make,
Insane the moment, sun just rose,
How many enemies, how many foes?
Bridges freeze, before the roads,
Who has the answer, is there a question?
Life is as simple as imagination,
Stomach is empty, kids have the flu,
Just lost your job, wife's angry with you,
Grocery prices are up; fuel 10 cents more, fill the truck,
Government will fix all the woes,
What do you mean our governments broke?
Float like a butterfly, swing on the tree,
Blinding snowstorm, no, sex isn't free,
Pay at the door, wait for the check,
Tip the waitress 20%;
Plan your life to prevail,
Missed that class in show and tell, smoke on the water, fireflies,
Lock the lap bar, enjoy the ride, ghosts are spirits all around,
Sweet bologna, $2.50 a pound,
I wish I were an Oscar Mayer wiener,
He is to fat; she wants to be thinner,
How many licks in a tootsie pop, the world may never know,
Need insurance save at Geico,
'Mommy can I have this Barbie'?
Made on the Main land, by the Chinese,
What has happened to the business structure?
Closing the gates of another manufacture,
Pray to God to make things better,
He stands by you in any weather,
Asked Him, for my mother to be saved,
We buried her yesterday,
For the best phone coverage get Verizon,
Clouds are gathering on the horizon,

I chose a career and obtained the knowledge,
Won't get this job, till I go back to college,
Fries, mashed, or baked potato,
Paper or plastic, to bag those?
Master degree to stock these shelves,
Break before 3, more pants to sell,
Get lunch at McDonalds, a number 2,
Need to hurry, use the drive thru,
A burger a fry and a coke, $6 bucks, what a joke,
'Plan to fly tomorrow; you're going to Tokyo',
"What, why are you sending me?"
'Because your resume said you knew Japanese',
'Konichiwa, that means hello and thanks, domo origato'
'That's all I've acquired…You lied to us, you're fired',
Plop plop, fizz fizz, oh what a relief it is,
Alka seltzer, I'll need some, the bar is empty, it's almost 1,
Coors light is the better beer, something's are unclear,
Alcohol takes lives if you chose to drink, accidents,
Destroys the liver, remember the prohibition,
The ads you won't forget,
Can't even buy them without permission,
Why can't you advertise a cigarette?
Chew Wrigley's gum, snickers snackradious, right?
You see the new commercial with Betty White,
Happy Birthday you're 21, congratulations you just had a son
40 years you worked to aspire
Can't believe you're going to retire
They say people are nicer if they own a cat,
Life's a bowl of cherries, imagine that…

Author…Dave Lord

Quiet love

Night blankets the day,
All the words are spoken,
On the bed we lay,
Our love is not yet broken,
Kiss upon your neck,
Chills stream down your back,
A night of silence, in a room of black,
Sparks into romance of slow intense heat,
Quietly our bodies come together,
Making love, lace to leather,
As the hours creep away,
Dawning, a new day,
Eyes glisten, smiles on our lips,
Warm under the covers,
Lovers share a kiss,
Quickly shower and dress for the job,
Your pillow holds a flower,
On your cheek a teardrop,
Breakfast made to order,
Hugs, we check the clock,
Dinner plans this evening,
That great Italian spot,
Each on our way,
The day about to start,
But knowing quiet love,
Held within our hearts…

Author…Dave Lord

Rain. . .

The rain begins, fog forms,
Upon the mist a teardrop falls,
Suffer no more, question not life's answers,
Swear at the storm, echoes from the mountain calls,
No longer, to seek the hearts roar,
Death you cannot serve,
Sun shines through the clouds to meet tomorrow,
Bow there to divine, forgive the sorrow,
Gifted are the lies left upon the doorstep,
Drift inside the eyes where the love is kept,
Sin can't disguise the colors of the, shadow
Walk and realize somewhere there's a rainbow…

Author…Dave Lord

Rainbow. . .

Search for a rainbow, on a cloudy afternoon,
Calling for a storm, in the middle of June,
Hoping for the sun to shine, pot of gold or just a dime,
Patience, until next time, comes darkness in the mind,
Silenced, no one will see, violence is the color,
Temple is complete, violins utter,
In a straw hat, farmer plows the fields,
Plant the seeds of wheat,
Don't look back, or to yield,
Bake some bread to eat,
I'm not my neighbor's keeper, they're vacationing,
They will return, sometime in the spring,
Hold to the future, the past has failed to try,
Fade to mature, sweet buy and buy,
Work the night shift, sleep during the day,
Get to make a living, die in distant gray,
Who will appreciate the red, the green, the indigo?
If you can't provide, where is the rainbow?
Coward, there you hide, orange and yellow and blue,
Sense of inner self, guide the mystic truth,
Get a coat its cold outside, snow begins to fall,
A dismal afternoon,
Catch a ride, baby learns to crawl,
Man on the moon,
Watch the TV show,
While waiting on a rainbow…

Author…Dave Lord

Restless. . .

Spirit lays beneath the ground, trying to escape,
Restless, wanting free, reliving each mistake,
Trapped inside the casket, buried there,
Begging for acceptance, truly scared,
Breaks the dawn in the east, sun climbs over the fog,
Priceless endeavor, smell the beast, searching for God,
Looking on the body, motionless,
Hoping to return from emptiness,
Children mourn the passing as the moments run,
Sibling steals the masses, the hour has begun,
Smoke upon the mystery, restless soul there next to me,
Treat the love respectably, could someone please pass the peas,
So many are hungry, drum the walls inside the box, think of fires,
Mend the socks, who is the liar, hide the rock,
Where in turn holds the key, bring the burgers that we may eat,
Trade the lover for the ball, pirouette, the candle falls,
Slip into the silent scream, spirit go and rest in peace…

Author…Dave Lord

Rise. . .

Rise with me to the air on a summer's noon,
Rise with me, skies are clear in a big balloon,
Climb above the trees, drift above life,
Feel the constant breeze, take away the strife,
Birds fly and sing, sun warms the skin,
Touch the eagle's wing, smile from within,
Noises from the city, cannot be heard,
Sights so pretty, submit and sense reward,
Tension from the body, releases to the wind,
Every moment passes, another one begins,
Arms around the waist, holding ever close,
Long is the embrace, tingle in the toes,
Lips cling together, sip the champagne,
Trip last forever; know my love to reign,
Clouds of puffy white float along beside,
I with you, my heart is filled with pride,
Ending with a jolt, the basket touches down,
Precious are the moments, together we are bound…

Author…Dave Lord

Ready to Fly...

The robin grows safe in its shell, protected
Slowly it breaks through, expected
Fed and nurtured before set free, ready to fly
Soon its' wings strong enough, freedom justified
As it soars toward the tree tops
Then down to the earth
Nearing the highway, rush twists the bird
Into a panic as trucks whisk by
The bird tumbles and lays to the side
Unknowing the stream of life was so quick
The bird takes to hiding, seemingly sick
Nests in the trees afraid to re-try
Protests his dreams, soon they die
Age creeps up as life passes by
His son questions, 'Dad, why don't we fly
I wish to soar like the other guys'
His father abruptly shares his fears
'You don't need to fly, just stay right here'
That night the son flaps his wings
Above the trees he starts to sing
The father nearly crippled with fright
Stares at the son by the moonlight
Suddenly the son begins to dive
The father afraid for his son's life
Soars into the air to meet his son
'Dad' the boy says, 'isn't this fun?'
The father realized he had faced his fears
Below the highway, the traffic, he peered
Understanding, as long as he flew high enough
The dangers of life, weren't so tough
And you can join the stream and merge into the hustle
Even if your feathers get ruffled
You pick yourself up and again you try
Enjoy your life....FLY!!!

Author...Dave Lord

169

Rose pedals. . .

Rose pedals on your bed; the room is dark and bare,
Turn your head to look around,
Yet no one is there,
Climb under the covers, a tug upon your hair,
A lick upon your cheek, you jump to your feet,
Checking the sheets, fear felt inside,
When you see, no one beside,
Lying down you turn out the light,
Belly trembles anxious of this night,
Soon your eyes close, sleep overtakes,
Summer breeze blows open the drapes,
First you feel the chill, then a warm sigh,
Your negligee removed, accept the sensual rise,
Restless is your body, in the summer's heat,
Emotions excited increase the hearts beat,
Hands upon the lipstick stain,
Back against the frame,
Squeeze the tube, cream squirts out,
Wipe it from your chin,
Grip the bed rail with a shout,
Plug the clock in,
Alarm buzzes, you're awake,
The bed is soaking wet,
Satisfied the night before,
The lover you've never met,
Like a dream you justify,
Your mind begins to settle,
Naked, reflects the mirrors glass,
Your breast, a rose pedal...

Author...Dave Lord

Sad

Near the door of absolute, waiting to get in,
Suddenly hear it close, maybe from the wind,
So I stand outside, the rain joins my tears,
Hoping just to be with you, the hours disappear,
Day is falling and dark is rushing in,
My heart is calling, drink a shot of gin,
Begging time to slow, sad in me begins,
Why can't I touch you, I long for your embrace,
The world seems to run through and steal my chance away,
Plans shattered, my moments of faith,
Will scattered, searching for grace,
Lifeless, my hands fall to the side,
Shoulders slump I hang my head to cry,
Turn my eyes toward heaven in despair,
Filled with passion I want to be there,
To see you smile, to hold you in my arms,
To touch an angel, elude stress filled harm,
From every day pressure, the weight crashing,
The oceans storm, the waves thrashing,
To calm peacefulness held within your eyes,
The sad lifts happiness arrives,
Sweet blissfulness chills down my back,
Surrender unto it sense of relax,
For a little while quest let it be,
Timeless happy hour with ecstasy...

Author...Dave Lord

Sadness. . .

Clouds above form, the rain will soon begin,
Hear the thunderstorm, time to go in
Teardrops from the angels, fall from their wings
Sad as they fall, still the earth sings,
For the drop of water helps renew the spring,
Plants accept nutrition, feeds then everything,
Then the summer sun heats all the rain,
Evaporates to steam, repeats it all again,
Teardrops from the angels, fall from their wings,
Sad as they fall, still the earth sings,
Though that of the angels falling from the sky,
Ever often sad is the lullaby, hearts they over fill,
Until the sad of angels, lovers often spill,
Sad among the presence, sad to fill the sigh,
Sad the effervescence, teardrops in the eyes,
Then makes one wonder, sad, reason why,
Answered by the lover, heard, the sad good bye,
Wondering, questioning, life, would it not be better,
Take from me my eyes, beauty can not see,
Take from me my voice, that may not speak,
Take from me my feelings, as lovers walk away,
Take from me my ears, no need to hear them say,
Words not honest, bitter is the taste,
Without flavor, food is but a waste,
Take from me living, for I need not breathe,
When it seems lovers, ever always leave,
Teardrops from the angels, fall from their wings,
Sad as they fall, still the earth sings...

Author...Dave Lord

Sailing. . .

Sailing on a memory, risking every scheme,
Driven by the sunset of calamity,
Waiting for the winter, chance to dot the eye,
Add a pinch of ginger, to the pumpkin pie,
Somewhere between deceit and ecstasy,
There you'll find a piece of purgatory,
Deliberately mistaken, there's the butterfly,
Sense the earth is shaken, above the clouded sky,
Love can't be found on a crooked road,
Silk from the parade upon the clay toad,
Passing through the town of Port Deposit,
Rail cars are full; coats are in the closet,
Hear the whiskey boys playing their bluegrass,
Johnny broke his arm, Suzy signed his cast,
Traffic on the highway, stop to pay the toll,
Cafeteria lunch today, tuna on a Kaiser roll,
Grab a bag of chips and an iced tea,
The meal will cost about $4.50,
Take the exit and stay to the right,
After 80 miles, time to get a bite,
Listen to the psychic read the tarot cards,
The future of the game depends upon the stars,
Will to make a fortune, photo opportunity,
Still the bride and groom, sailing on a memory...

Author...Dave Lord

So much time. . .

So much time, make a plan,
At the beach, in the sand,
Tomorrows, tomorrow, future is near,
Plan the next day, year after year,
So many months in advance,
Today never gets a second chance,
Precious the moment, savor it too,
Many moments, to choose,
The sun will rise, whether you care or not,
Behind grey skies the sun burns hot,
Grain after grain the sand disappears,
Life, emotion, laughter and tears,
At anytime the sand in your grip,
Could fall right through, eventually sift,
Then all which you held in your hand,
Drifts and joins the other sand,
As life itself,
Think of others more than yourself,
Holding on as long as you can,
In a blink of an eye, understand,
Life slips through,
That's when you notice those moments were few...

Author...Dave Lord

Satin Sheets. . .

Lie upon the satin sheets, close your eyes, relax,
Rose pedals hair to feet, room tense with sex,
Music playing softly, love songs, violins,
Lights are turned off, candles flickering,
Naked as we lay, the scent of your perfume,
The taste of lemon drops, in the darkened room,
Your mouth around the feast, the pudding overflows,
In the summer's heat, passion ever grows,
Squeeze the milk and honey, lick what's left behind,
Slice the berry pie, hear the coffee grind,
Lost in sweet affection, sprayed by sparkling wine,
Wipe the beaded brow; try to catch your breath,
Ever willing, to perform the test, strengthen the mixture,
Turn the doors knob, grip the solid fixture,
Feel the hearts throb, caress the peaches,
Deep, the French kiss, tongue the cherry's juices,
Excess on the lips, bite the apple, delicious and red,
Joyous sensations fill the head, sprawled out lifeless,
Searching for wind, exhausted,
Contagious…skin on skin…

Author…Dave Lord

Saturated. . .

Saturated by discontentment of life,
Complicated by trying to earn a living,
Saturated with disappointment and the strife,
Hope this God is one of forgiving,
Vindicated by trails and tribulations,
Hell resides with loves indignation,
Sling the mud, wait, anticipation,
Signified by the media's operation,
Kill the tried because of indication,
Day to day buried in frustration,
Stride by stride feel the, inhibition
Dealing with the daily aggravation,
Wondering what is the destination,
Frightened by the experts calculations,
Teacher can you teach us education,
Justified, the tears of salutation,
In the lies seek appreciation,
Worry not of the explanation,
Moments of will, show determination,
Broken still, by the power of manipulation,
Where's the thrill, controlled population,
Rush the hill, you greedy generation,
Buy the pills to help your concentration,
Hear them drill the minds of preparation,
Drink the swill you fools who vacation,
Bend the rules you larger corporations,
Blessings fill the churches congregations,
Pay the bill; you bought your preservation,
Tend to the sheep, uphold the situation,
It's the weak, who fail, insinuation,
Mountain steep, defeated, interpretation,
See the creek, rise to the occasion,
Cut inside the knife makes the incision,
Often cry due to the depression,
Torn apart by the segregation,
Burn alive, sense incineration,
Learn to fly reincarnation,

Touch the sky, there is the translation,
Time ticks by, sin and damnation,
Then to die, assassination,
Breached is the desperation,
Soul is wise, join in the accession…

Author
Dave Lord

Scent. . .

Touch the scent of in between
Savor the musk of June
Hold the lover in your arms
In the afternoon
Sense the heat of passion
Breed the summer night
Felt in timely fashion
Lust has taken flight
Drink the milk of solitude
Plant the sunflower seed
Share the sexual prelude
Intense is the need
Care for one another
Kiss upon the rose
Dare to fondle trouble
Excite the flower grows
Then until tomorrow
Time will pass on by
Trust the wind to follow
Come precious, nigh…

Author…Dave Lord

Shadow. . .

Through the window a shadow, no one is there,
Call your name, death will not share,
Life ever after, afterlife,
Time is the blade, which cuts like a knife,
Into the future, not healing the past,
Try to capture smiles when they're cast,
Aimlessly wonder, still seeking love,
Heaven or hell release this numb,
Tormented heartache covered in blood,
Hell hath no fury, heavenly son,
Opinions of how the bible reads,
Truths are the lies we choose to believe,
Reach for a photo shed one more tear,
Wait for the shadows to reappear,
Life resurrected year after year,
Time the expectant that pain disappears,
Though reluctant the endless task,
Relentless, forward, put on the mask,
Say good-bye to lover and friend,
Tomorrow calls, today brings its end…

Author…Dave Lord

Silent Night. . .

Silent nights, fantasies
Peace filled flight, Damocles'
Endless dreams, cast out to sea
When will the hair break?
Whose soul is charged?
Why doest thou take?
Dead becomes the heartbeat
Anger in the mind
Bitch, will not speak
Wait another time
Excuses, I have heard
Months have passed on by
Whore, is the word
Sensed behind the eye
Low and behold
There comes a symphony
Warmth from the cold
Soon there will be
There you will lie
In a den of thieves
Love, again to die
Hell within me…

Author…Dave Lord

Silent Slaughter. . .

In the night, silent slaughter,
Warn your sons and hide your daughters,
Clash of the warriors has been ordered,
Gentle misfortune swells in the seas,
Heard from the voice of Galilee,
Hold to tomorrow, carry your swords,
Beg, steal, or borrow forbidden words,
Stand and do battle before you fall,
With bow and arrow scale the walls,
Heard from a distance the quiet screams,
Time to awaken from your dream,
Take up the shield, defend till death,
Hide in the fields with your bullet proof vest,
Shower the enemy with shells from above,
Who forms the wicked with failing love,
Who then decides the evil being?
Judge is then judged, isn't he?
Lift your weapon and kill this foe,
Drink the toast of desperate woe,
Find the devil wherever you go,
Hide the knowledge, if they don't know,
Drag the waters for life itself,
Silent slaughter, a wishing well,
Blood for blood, tooth and nail,
As the crypt keeper soon prevails,
Break the stones and spare the rod,
Children grow too seek their God,
Banish all who welcome sin,
Hell awaits, let them in...

Author...Dave Lord

181

The Aging of Time. . .

The aging of time, the hours pass away,
The aging of time, day after day,
The aging of time, the years carry on,
The aging of time, dusk until dawn,
The aging of time, reflects the mirrored glass,
The aging of time, time is the past,
The aging of time, purposeful it seems,
The aging of time, destroys all the dreams,
The aging of time, careful as it goes,
The aging of time, the glass ever shows,
The aging of time, what is wished to be,
The aging of time, only grants reality,
The aging of time, come knock upon the door,
The aging of time, stopped... ever more.

Author...Dave Lord

Tonic. . .

Rain upon the shadow, punch upon the chin,
Sit on the patio with a tonic and gin,
Mindless conversation spoken opinions,
Hear that fat girl wish she was slim,
Whiskey drinking woman at the town hall,
Tarp upon the window, traffics at a crawl,
What's the definition, where's the crystal ball,
Fuck determination, wish and get it all,
Fantasies happen, time to make the sale,
Crack open the Captain, hear the tinker bell,
Drive the crying stripper to the chapel,
Hide inside the bubble, never see the real,
20 men begging at the local grill,
Standing at the corner waiting for the food,
20 vultures ready for the kill,
Car pulls in the driveway, like the birds of prey,
Swoop upon the carcass, survive another day,
Lady in a beat up 15 year old car,
Brings groceries to help them get this far,
Hand upon the bible, foot upon the grass,
The earth is still unstable, kicked in the ass,
Grab a piece of heaven, stumble as they run,
Draw the Smith and Wesson, bullet from the gun,
Another body lying in the filthy street,
Over simplifying, dead because of beef,
Is the world relying, man will self destruct,
Economic turns because the mighty buck,
Don't worry, no need to panic,
Time to shift the deck chairs on the Titanic...

Author - Dave Lord

183

Unanswered...

How can one be satisfied
When unanswered are his dreams
When he calls to heaven, down on bended knees
The hopes of tomorrow, the wishes of today
Disappointed his sweet sorrow
Never reached to his dismay
Requests to see the mountains
The peaks of joyfulness
Stops when life ends, unanswered happiness
Then all the words of promise
Spoken with faith
Failed, and those who hear them
Disbelief upon their face
Wealth one has trusted
To be his upon this earth
The quest surely broken
Cast aside is his worth
All held in wait with God, unanswered
All that trust placed in the ground
Along with the dreams...poor bastard.

Author...Dave Lord

Vampire. . .

Well another lesson learned
As I add on the age, there is no return
The years keep running away
Though I now understand why
A younger woman is sought by an older guy
First there is the innocence; she won't kill your ego
Their willingness, they don't often say "No"
Enjoying the moment of which life brings
Not trying to pull on your heartstrings
Free spirited, not planning to conspire
Making older men into vampires
Once you taste the young, there is no turning back
The transition begun, you hunt your next attack
Searching for a victim, inside you know it's not right
Society would cast you aside, but the felling of strength and might
You quickly swallow your pride you do what is selfish
Not caring what is said
You hear your heartbeat, realize you're not dead
You look for another, a quest for the feast
Adrenalin rush, you feel like a beast
There one sits, nearing the hour
Last call for the night, you feel empowered
Her intoxication working for you
She is yours tonight, lies become truths
The hour strikes, she is there in your bed
The sensual evening spins in your head
A vampire renewed by the blood
Cursed I am, for I tasted the young...

Author...Dave Lord

Trapped emotions. . .

Trapped emotions can't you see,
Life is more than work,
Love is what I want to bleed,
Time erasing worth,
Will to echo silently,
Breathe the dust and dirt,
Send a sign that I believe,
Born of this rebirth,
Bells are ringing constantly,
Fades another day,
Hold the tissue while you sneeze,
Wipe the tears away, drink the whiskey sour,
Paint the walls hot pink, scratch the old mans whiskers,
Excitement on the brink, eyes stare at the statue,
Goddess standing there, flesh enjoy the virtue,
Sight lures respect, arms around the pillar,
Held in place erect, slip into the gown,
Plant another seed, tie the tension down,
Passion grip the feet, clip the weeping willow,
Branch is in the hand, scream into the pillow,
Drummer in a band,
Lick the ice cream from the wafer cone,
Caress the roses pedals, bucked, the horsemen thrown,
Sweat upon the brow, the taste of pure delight,
Restless is the vow, sleepless is the night…

Author…Dave Lord

Warrior. . .

Deep inside the darkened secret, where no one can see,
Reckoned intervention, blind in front of me,
Warrior surface, redeem thyself, holier then thou,
Wreckage goes before, serve thy kingdom now,
Though the mind is filled with doubt,
Taught to know what is good,
Love another is cast out, yet, the war stood,
Still feel the tension, fear the inner child,
Take up your weapon, survive the beast of wild,
Justify the action, at the churches door,
There the attraction, peace...warrior,
Restless indignation, death is upon me,
Seek the path of present, instability,
Look there behind, watch the wicked fall,
Who then is kind, blood spattered walls,
Smoke a cigarette, read the scripture words,
Above you, flies a jet, air raid sirens heard,
'Are they of those for the greater good'?
Foe to foe, life misunderstood,
Back inside the office, Generals there decide,
Whose blood is yours, take it all in stride,
Box another human, sent to a grave,
Judging what is done, leader of the brave,
Counteract the senseless, laws, ours from before,
See the devastation war, means more...

Author...Dave Lord

Satin Sheets. . .

Lie upon the satin sheets, close your eyes, relax,
Rose pedals hair to feet, room tense with sex,
Music playing softly, love songs, violins,
Lights are turned off, candles flickering,
Naked as we lay, the scent of your perfume,
The taste of lemon drops, in the darkened room,
Your mouth around the feast, the pudding overflows,
In the summer's heat, passion ever grows,
Squeeze the milk and honey, lick what's left behind,
Slice the berry pie, hear the coffee grind,
Lost in sweet affection, sprayed by sparkling wine,
Wipe the beaded brow; try to catch your breath,
Ever willing, to perform the test, strengthen the mixture,
Turn the doors knob, grip the solid fixture,
Feel the hearts throb, caress the peaches,
Deep, the French kiss, tongue the cherry's juices,
Excess on the lips, bite the apple, delicious and red,
Joyous sensations fill the head, sprawled out lifeless,
Searching for wind, exhausted,
Contagious…skin on skin…

Author…Dave Lord

The Tear. . .

The tear falls from my chin,
Hear the silent whisper; I hold your hand,
Outside dogs bark, two shadows glide across the wind,
I stretch to kiss her, song from the band,
Catch the shooting star, walk beside the ocean,
Drive the interstate, what's all the commotion,
Bar is closing its getting late, touch the scent of loveliness,
Break the plate glass window; show them all you're fearless,
Weakened by the day, nice feather pillow,
Soul about to fray, drunken fool take it easy,
All is vague, who shall I please, Sunday time for church,
Cook the pot of soup, bread about to burn, grab the pool cue,
Then fell across the room a hush, visit the elderly, embarrassed
Some blush, in the distance a Harley, what's the weather for tomorrow,
Buy a pink rose, no money can I borrow, time for another dose,
He seems disturbed, finger tips tap, excuse me I burped,
About to collapse, heart rate is normal, blood pressure is high,
The dance is formal, where the white tie, package on the porch,
Rain has soaked my shirt, light the torch, sad filled with hurt,
Press the green button, precious little girl, coin thrown in the fountain,
Peanut for the squirrel, quiet expression, skies are clear and blue,
So much expectation, lips are chapped, stepping through,
Want to take a nap, wet summer dew, must wind the clock,
Charter boats crew waits by the dock, justified in the news,
Dignified obeys every law, children running nude,
Lean against the wall, find the missing link,
Taste the apple pie, stand upon the brink,
Light the candle say good bye...

Author...Dave Lord

That. . .

I have given you all that,
Which you may build upon,
Darling, if you please,
Dance upon the boulevard,
Then get on your knees,
Pray to the living God, Master if you will,
Bless this home and all inside, punctuate the kill,
The word has promised, no more shall be a flood,
Water levels rising, take a pint of blood,
Ice caps are melting, Father did you lie?
'No child, this flood is not of mine,'
Answer, what then should we do?
'I am not the problem world, this time it is you',
Cease the moment, earth and wind and sky,
Rivers movement, control the beast and ride,
Money is the enemy, survival is the need,
Greed is the demon, growing like a weed,
Give a dime per dollar, one tenth if you would,
Selfish individual, carnal knowledge understood,
Sermons of the muddy winter, summer freeze the pipes,
Spring the leaves drop like butter, fall there bigger flies,
Sun is ever warmer, cold is much to brisk,
Poison one another, Persuade to eat the fish;
Drivers start your engines; have to earn your keep,
Then the earth surrenders,
'Will you feed my sheep?'
Jesus is the secret…ever all do sleep

Author…Dave Lord

190

Tunnel. . .

Into the tunnel, I'm heading in
Darkness surrounds me fear begins
Through the tunnel, the other side
Light gleaming, I need not hide
New experience, challenge, await me there
So I work through the tunnel with less despair
The other side, I see the light
The other side I feel fresh life
No matter the task, which brings me through
To myself I must be true
Each endeavor brings new height
Faster my travels toward the light
When I've achieved passing through
Another tunnel I must do
Birth, education, work
Career, family, marriage, divorce
Each tunnel is a course
Knowledge, love, learning, leading
Each tunnels gift is worth receiving
One more tunnel I must go through
A light ahead, new life...I do...

Author
David Lord

Voices. . .

Voices in the head…more like screams,
Louder in the bed, invading the dreams,
Judge not the soul, can you not hear,
Damned there, behold, the blood, the sweat, the fear,
Tempt the lips of Satan, lost the generosity,
See the road less taken, heard the prophecy,
Sleep, failed, awaken, time is longevity,
Pour another whiskey; drink until passed out,
Saved the crimes which could be, Knights begin to joust,
Thy against thyself, so that thou believe,
Tomorrow no one else, bitten by the beast,
Words upon a rumor, resonance in the clouds,
Feel the wooden splinter, curse the well endowed,
Broken 'ever after', sounds of long good-byes,
Syndicate catastrophe, next the children cry,
Forever be forgotten, history be gone,
Today we sell what's rotten, soon another dawn,
Send it to the sinful, fall unto the floor,
Betrayed are the forgiven, make another rule,
How long must one wait across the great divide,
There's another earthquake, off the western shore,
Are we truly living, who is the fool, taste the cyanide,
Sorry, to give so much harm, so little right,
Identify the scars; don't want to fight,
Enter the dragon, pink are the skies, circle the wagons, step on the flies,
Burden the pope, in the Vatican, where is hope, the sun is getting dim,
Beautiful lady, under her clothes, naked redemption head to toe,
Run for the roses, carry the cup, build on supposes, under the rug,
Listen to silence, look toward the moon,
Bury the ignorance, golden spoon…

Author…Dave Lord

What Reason. . .

What reason have I to live, the world is so unkind,
The hours, to work I give, no money do I find,
Take away the evidence of life that I should bleed,
Smell the sense of timelessness, can you taste the breed,
Though my heart takes on the shield, though I beg to plead,
Wanting, to break the yield, of sexuality,
Thrust the hammer upon the lust, feel the summers heat,
Cage the lover, where's the trust, come, and know complete,
Charge the despicable yesterday, tempt tomorrow's cheek,
Flow the blessed passions, terrorize the mystic,
No more to ration, put on the lipstick,
In a suit of bronze, ecstasy beyond,
Feel the massage, naked as you lay,
Not a facade, shape the potters clay,
Mouth upon the dream, sunrise comes along,
Coffee with some cream, brisk the eyes of dawn,
Daylight brings the enemy, there upon its needs,
Sell the cup of greed, yet of loves delight, will it ever be,
Alone the clock ticks, hell ignites the beauty,
Camera aim and click, share the fantasy,
View the reason, may I breathe?
Set the soul free...

Author...Dave Lord

Tough. . .

Are you really that tough?
Or is it just a facade,
To protect from the pain, we've all been victim of,
Get in the face of your adversary,
Make the mistake of adversity,
Could this conflict have been avoided?
Tales of the dead have been recorded,
Often thought by the invincible,
Nothing could they loose,
As stated at their burial,
Sad the misjudgment they choose,
'Laws were made to be broken' the motto of the jails,
Handcuff marks are the token,
And money for lawyers and bail,
It is not a tax write off,
Nor a business expense,
So for that moment of stupid,
Comes this period of intense,
Strain on the wallet, relation or family,
Years to regain a trust,
Doesn't make sense logically,
To stir up so much dust,
So if in a situation,
Where what you choose could be illegal,
No need for speculation,
Say 'no thanks' and welcome frugal…

Author…Dave Lord

194

Stillness. . .

In the stillness of the dead,
As you wring your hands red,
Silent is the night,
Holding on to tight,
Fearing the streets, feel the echoes repeat,
Waiting for a slow ride, building a stable, hide,
Changing the rules, sleeping with bulls,
Stealing hope to believe, siding for the reprieve,
Staying with the hostel, reading the gospel,
Loving much to little, drinking from the whiskey bottle,
Trying to be heard, wanting the bullets toll,
Listening to rock and roll,
Ranting about the days genius,
Whether it's controlled by a pussy or a penis,
Who does it save, how will it help,
It's time to shave, heard the belch,
Could lose a few pounds, restlessly bored,
Whatever you seek, bound to score,
Dinner was too cheap,
Part of the university, life has its adversity,
Wet, the pavements illness,
This defines the stillness...

Author...Dave Lord

Treadmill. . .

There was a time not long ago life could be enjoyed,
Now we have these rules everyone's annoyed,
I remember when bills I could pay,
Now years have gone by without a raise,
Though gas went up half a dollar,
Bread and milk too, electric and water,
Have gone through the roof,
Taxes just came in they're much higher,
And the cell phone, that bill is on fire,
It used to cost a quarter to make a local call,
Now $300 a month, damn it all,
The paycheck is getting spread to thin,
Late with one payment, and a fee is given,
$40.00 charge when the bill is 30 bucks,
Ever pushing deeper, WTF!,
Credit score is tainted, can't afford the car,
I nearly fainted, in life I'm not that far,
No money in savings, no 401k plan,
After this 20 dollars, I'm a broke man,
Can't afford the whiskey, life has lost its thrill,
I'd really like to know, how to get off this treadmill...

Author...Dave Lord

Who. . .

Who do I follow, heaven or hell?
On this earthly plain,
Under who's spell?
I follow the direction of the holy word,
But on my weakly path,
I wonder who I serve,
Often weakened of the flesh,
Sometimes defeated, such a wreck,
Sin and sex what I want to own,
Is hell the misery, I will call home?
I look to the bible, fall onto my knees,
Tomorrow a sinner, life is the disease,
Though the word states
God knows my every plan,
All that I wish is of the simple man,
The love of a woman, and a family,
Survive just a little, requesting, please,
A home, happy welcomed equally,
The beautiful woman there for me,
Enjoy the laughter, while each tick of time,
Towards ever after sweetly I oblige…

Author…Dave Lord

Young Man. . .

Young man rushes in, announcing his plan,
Expressing his life to be a business man,
His father hears his son's words, dare he not consider,
To crush his sons dream, so he'll not become a quitter,
Listening intently encouraging, tries to imply his voice of reason,
The son hears damaging, unknown his fathers seasons,
Where he too walked in his sons' pride,
Echoing… "Why do you not believe in me?
I have so much to offer, I'm off on my own,
I'll make it, you'll see, father,"
Years come and go, time passes by,
Life as we know, teaches while we try,
Lessons have been taught, a man of all seasons,
A father to his son, a new voice of reason,
'Well dad I'm ready, got myself a plan,
Going to start my life, going to be a man,
Got myself a job, new car, a girl to wed,
Wish me well, that's all that need be said'
Father hears, the voice in his mind repeating,
But stops himself, instead begins praying
'God, my son, please, will you bless him'…

Author…Dave Lord

Vanity

The course we chose is all in vain,
Still our minds reach the pain,
As we quietly go insane,
Work like dogs as we try,
Freedom sought like birds to fly,
Yet often nights our heart does cry,
Drag the demons to the south,
Preach the righteous from your mouth,
Hide the secrets in your house,
Bless the damned, hell is taught,
Earn the cross, man has bought,
Damn the blessing, no one caught,
Seek the justice in your mind,
Ask the judgment be defined,
Realize the judge has died,
Tell the world to be patient,
Wonder why life swiftly went,
Curse successes never sent,
Write the checks from each pay,
Feel the stress each burning day,
Reflection shares its touch of gray,
Speak your lies convince as truth,
Recognize the past was youth,
Tomorrow's wealth is overdue,
As we quicken loves pace,
Another soul goes to waste,
No longer will she wait,
Blackened nights of all alone,
Hear the sounds the sobbing tones,
Reaching depths of the unknown,
Mystified your chest is tight,
Touch the warmth dawns breaking light,
Sanctified, the end is life,

Author...Dave Lord

Whisper. . .

Whisper in a crowded room, hear the warm hello,
Crave a secluded June, your head upon the pillow,
Tantalized by the wanting view, inside my mind where I see you,
Crimson fire out of control, can you touch the flames,
Where desire plays the roll, sensual, just the same,
Body of a goddess lies across the stream,
Bridge to paradise, somewhere in between,
Lace upon the breasts, leather are the jeans,
Water near to crest, torn about the seams,
Jagged is the broken glass, sharp the two edged sword,
Time will never cease to pass; my dreams are filled with words,
Cast out the demons, pray the angels come,
Another night is screaming, the mountain peaks, the sun,
Filled with aspiration, to late to say good bye,
To hell with the decisions of a fear to fly,
Bring around the limousine, drive to the club,
Photos in the magazine, celebrate the pub,
Drink another tequila, smoke the cigarette,
The ice cream is vanilla, wish for no regrets,
Then to see the road of yellow bricks,
Follow to forever, lover do not quit,
Sneak on the horizon, the future can not know,
The heat we rely on is needed when it snows...

Author...Dave Lord

Unwanted. . .

There comes a time in life, when age becomes the enemy,
And hell becomes the price, of youth's iniquity,
Suddenly what was, is now what used to be,
Less wanted you become; there is a lesser need,
The spouse you've loved, has grown apart,
The children you think of, they depart,
Independent, on their own, how you brought them up,
The distant unknown, stop at the local pub,
To drown your sorrows,
Holding on to what makes you feel alive,
A new tomorrow, 30 years working 8 to 5,
Only to find a slip in your pay,
End of the week is your last day,
Out of work, kids are gone,
Wife doesn't care, and dreams are torn,
Wishing for hope, hoping for strength,
Grasping at straws, trying to catch a thrill,
Begging the Gods to show you faith,
Wondering if you have the will,
Together the 2 of you can survive,
But is it worth the sacrifice,
Introduced to a blanket of woes,
Find your friends have turned to foe,
Tumble from the ladder you've climbed,
Close your eyes to the sublime,
Worry your beliefs are just a lie,
Another generation taught,
Again desperation brought,
Blinded by the blow, daunted,
Realize you're unwanted…

Author…Dave Lord

Wings. . .

Brush the wings of criminal,
Brush the wings of death,
Realize life is critical,
Enjoy every breath,
Care for one another,
Put forth all your love,
Don't forget to kneel to the God above,
You receive a living, but you give a life,
Always be forgiving, learn from all the hype,
Inside reaping, time is the price,
As the clock is ticking, as the numbers rise,
The body takes the licking, age is the surprise,
Moments of anger piercing, each creates a hole,
Slowly faith is shrinking, damaging the soul,
Ever looking forward, always looking up,
May Gods blessings save you from hells cusp,
Look inside ones self, release the suffering,
May the worlds touch cause your heart to sing,
On your way, towards angel's wings…

Author…Dave Lord

Worry. . .

Worry, fills my days
Fear comes in the night
Money, there's not enough
Life, I lose the fight
But I know as long as I'm awake
There is hope and I'll have faith
Or fall to this worlds defeat
For I know this war I can beat
Another day another month
Another year and time will come
Where the wave that covers me
Will pull back into the sea
Then I'll stand upon my feet
And I'll brush the sand off my seat
I'll walk ever tall
To life I will not fall
For my God has a plan for me
I will reflect the light for thee

Author...Dave Lord